S0-CCE-935

Happy Moments With God

Alum Rock Covenant Church
218 KIRK AVENUE
S N JOSE 27, CALIFORNIA

Happy Moments With God

Devotions
Especially Written
For Families With
Young Children

Margaret Anderson

Bethany Fellowship, Inc.
Minneapolis, Minnesota

Tenth Printing (newly illustrated)— 1973

BETHANY FELLOWSHIP, INC.
6820 Auto Club Road
Minneapolis, Minnesota 55438

Cover Photo: Armstrong-Roberts
Inside Photos: John Thornberg
and James Pope

Printed in the United States of America

Dedicated to
MY HUSBAND
*in grateful appreciation for his
encouragement and love*

INTRODUCTION

Dear Mother and Dad,

This book was written to help you keep a devotional time with your children.

Their needs and interests conditioned the vocabulary and anecdote choice. You will note, too, that some of the Bible passages are paraphrased to make them more easily understood.

There may be instances, however, where you will need to explain concepts about which questions are asked.

Though many of the illustrations are actual experiences of my own children, I am grateful to friends who allowed me to use experiences in which their youngsters were involved.

I know God will bless you as you challenge your loved ones to live for Him.

MARGARET J. ANDERSON

CONTENTS

A Place in Your Heart

Miss Ames, Becky's Sunday school teacher, had told the children in her class about Jesus. She showed them a picture of Jesus knocking at a door. The door didn't have any latch or doorknob on the outside. That meant it had to be opened from the inside by the people who lived in the house.

Miss Ames told the children Jesus knocks at their heart door in the same way. Then she said that no matter how young they were, they could invite Jesus to come and live in their hearts.

Many of the boys and girls did this. Becky asked Jesus to come into her heart, too.

Yet, because she was so very young, she didn't quite understand how this could be.

She decided she would ask Daddy. He always explained things so well.

"So that's what has been troubling you," Daddy said as he lifted Becky into his lap. "Well, let's think of it this way. Do you remember when Aunt Grace and Uncle Tom adopted little Timmy?"

Becky nodded.

"Do you remember when we visited them a few months later?" Becky nodded again.

"One of the first things Aunt Grace said was, 'We don't know what we would do without him. He has certainly made a big place for himself in our hearts.' Now that didn't mean that Timmy had crawled inside of Aunt Grace's heart, did it?"

Becky shook her head. She was beginning to understand.

"Then what do you think it meant?"

Becky thought for awhile. Then she said,

"I think it meant that they loved him a whole lot."

"That's right," Daddy said. "Now this question, do I have a place in your heart, Becky?"

Becky snuggled close to her Daddy.

"You know you do," she said. Then looking at him slyly, she asked,

"And do I have a place in your heart, Daddy?"

"You know you do," Daddy told her. "You and the Lord Jesus, too."

Something to Think About: Have you ever wondered what it meant to give your heart to Jesus? Have you wondered what it meant to have Him come into your heart? Now you know it really means that you love Him a great deal.

When Jesus comes into your life He has an important place in your heart.

Bible Verse: "That Christ may live in your hearts by faith [believing love]" (Ephesians 3:17).

"God has sent the Spirit of His Son into your hearts" (Galatians 4:6).

Prayer: Dear Father above, once again we thank You for sending Your Son to live in our hearts. Keep our hearts clean and pure for Him. In His Name we pray. Amen.

How Old?

"Mummy?" It was little Sheryl Anne who spoke.

"Yes, dear," Mother answered.

Sheryl Anne sat on the floor in her mother's sewing room. Though she had been playing with her dolls, Mother knew something was bothering her.

"Mummy," she began again. "How old do I need to be before I can give my heart to Jesus?"

Mother put the dress she was sewing on the sewing machine.

"Come here, dear," she said.

Sheryl ran to her mother. She climbed into her lap.

"How old do you need to be to love me?" Mother asked.

Sheryl wrinkled her forehead. Mother could tell she was thinking about the question.

"I love you now," Sheryl said.

"Good," Mother answered. "And, how old do you have to be to love Daddy?"

This time the answer came quickly.

"But, Mummy, I love him now."

"All right, Sheryl, one more question. How old do you have to be to love baby brother?"

"Mummy, you know," Sheryl told her. "You know I love him now."

"And do you love Jesus?"

"Of course."

"Then I am sure you are old enough to give Him your heart. And you can do it right now. Just fold your hands and tell Jesus that you love Him and want to belong to Him always."

Something to Think About: Sheryl bowed her head, folded her hands and told Jesus that she loved Him. She invited Jesus to come into her heart.

You see, no one is too young to give Jesus his heart. No one is too old either.

But, the Bible tells us it is wise to do this while we are young so that when we are older we will always want to live for Him.

Have you given Jesus your heart?

15

Bible Verse: "Choose you this day whom ye will serve . . . but as for me and my house [children] we will serve the Lord" (Joshua 24:15).

Prayer: Dear Lord Jesus, we thank You that we can love You while we are still young. Keep us in that love. In Jesus' Name. Amen.

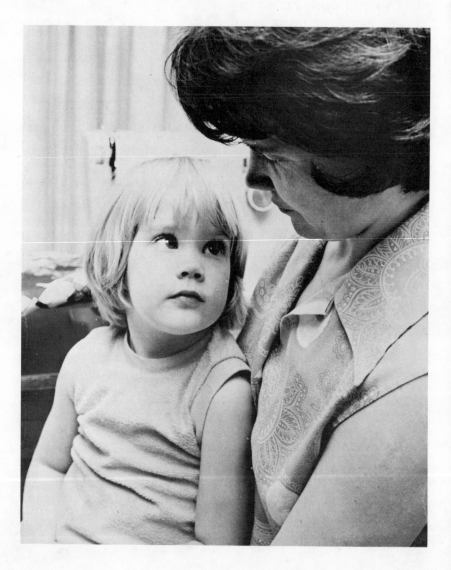

Deep, Deep in the Sea

Have you ever been in a boat or on a dock when someone put a long pole into the water to see how deep the water was?

Usually this distance measures only a few feet. Big oceans, though, are many miles deep. In fact, just a few years ago the United States Navy found the deepest place in the whole world.

It isn't in the middle of the Atlantic Ocean. It isn't in the middle of the Pacific Ocean. The deepest spot is found in the Philippine Sea. If you were going to see how deep it is at that spot, you would have to have a pole six and a half miles long! Someone has said twenty-seven Empire State buildings could be stacked one on top of the other and the last one would still be under water. It is that deep.

If you dropped a penny into the water, it would take several hours for it to reach bottom.

That's mighty deep, isn't it?

Something to Think About: Do you know why it is interesting to know how deep the deepest spot in the world is? Perhaps you have never thought about this before. But, when we read what Micah, an Old Testament prophet, said about the depth of the sea, we understand why it is important to us. He said our sins are cast into the depth of the sea. And when he says that, we know just how far away they are.

Yet, this doesn't mean that all our sins lie on the bottom of the ocean floor. Rather, it shows that God puts them out of His mind — that He remembers them no more.

Bible Verse: "He will forgive our sins and will cast them into the depths of the sea" (Micah 7:19).

"I am God who blotteth out your sins and remembers them no more" (Isaiah 43:25).

Prayer: Dear Heavenly Father, we thank You for sending Your Son, Jesus, to this earth. We thank You because we know He forgives us our sins. We thank You because You have promised to blot them out (to cast them into the depths of the sea); and because You have promised not to remember them anymore. In Jesus' Name. Amen.

To Forgive Is to Forget

Joey Nelson sat on the back steps pouting. Mother stood by the kitchen door watching him. Joey could tell she knew something was wrong. "Well, Joey," she said. "Why such a long face on such a beautiful morning?"

"I'm mad!" he answered, his chin set angrily in his cupped hands.

"At whom?" Mother wanted to know.

"At Terry." He almost growled the words.

"And why?" She *would* ask that.

"You remember," Joey answered. "He broke my bike chain and now I've got to sit here until it's fixed."

"Come, come," Mother chided as she stepped through the door and walked down the steps to where Joey was sitting. "Terry said he was sorry. And it seems to me I heard you say you would forgive him."

"Sure, but I didn't know the kids were going to ride their bikes to the park today. Dad said he couldn't fix the chain until tonight. If Terry hadn't broken the chain, I could be with the kids now."

"And, you're going to sit here and pout about it all day?" Mother asked. "Say, maybe you need a lesson in what forgiveness really means."

Joey didn't answer. He just scowled and scuffed his shoe back and forth on the sidewalk.

"Wait here," Mother told him. "We'll have that lesson right now."

In a few minutes she was back with Joey's slate, a piece of chalk and an eraser.

Once again she sat down beside Joey. She placed the eraser on the step and began to draw. Joey edged closer so he could see what she drew. As long as he could remember, Mother had been drawing pictures for him. She was good at it, too.

But Mother didn't intend that Joey should watch. She turned Joey's face away from the slate.

"You can't look yet," she told him.

Joey waited. He heard the quick fast strokes of the chalk on the slate. He wondered what kind of a lesson she could teach him with a picture. Then he thought about his bicycle again. He bit his lips and clenched his fist. He'd get even with Terry for breaking the chain.

"Now," Mother whispered and Joey knew it was time for him to look. Joey turned. The picture was finished. It was almost like a funny paper picture. There was his bike, lying topsy-turvy by the sidewalk, wheels in the air, a broken chain dangling in the grass.

And there was Terry, shirt out of his pants, brushing the dust and dirt off his arms and legs.

Joey couldn't help but smile. Mother surely knew how to make her pictures like real life.

"Now," Mother began, "remember what happened after Terry had the accident? He said he was sorry, didn't he?"

19

As Terry nodded, Mother drew a big cross mark through the picture. "There, now he's forgiven, like you said. Okay?"

Joey nodded again. He couldn't understand what his mother was trying to show him.

"Now suppose I hang this picture in your room. Every day you look at it. Do you think you will ever forget about the broken chain?"

"No. . . ." Joey answered slowly.

"Well, memory is really a picture in the mind. As long as you hold on to it and keep thinking about it, you'll keep seeing it. Here," she stopped talking and handed Joey the eraser. "Show me how to get rid of that picture."

Joey hated to spoil the picture but he did what he knew his mother wanted him to. He rubbed the slate with the eraser. A few quick strokes back and forth, and the picture was gone.

"Now do you see there's a lot of difference between saying you forgive someone and then forgetting the wrong was ever there?"

Joey didn't say anything for a long time. Then all of a sudden he stood up. "Guess I'll walk over to the park," he said. "I can play with the kids even if I can't ride with them." He knew this would be the quickest and best way to cross the picture from his mind.

Something to Think About: Do we really forgive if we don't forget? What is the best way to forget a wrong? Sometimes it helps to think about something else when we want to cross a picture out of our mind. Think of something good about the person who wronged you. Pray for that person. Ask God to bless him.

Bible Verse: "I am He that erased thy sins and remembered them no more" (Isaiah 43:25).

Prayer: Dear Father in heaven, we thank You for sending Your Son to this world to die for us. We thank You that He set an example for us when He taught us to forgive. Help us to say, "Forgive them because they didn't mean to do wrong." And help us to forget when we forgive. In Jesus' Name. Amen.

A Little Honey

One day Patty came running into the kitchen. She wrinkled her nose and sniffed the air.

"Yummy! That smells good. What is it?" she asked.

"A hot dish that's baking in the oven," Mother told her.

"Are we going to have it for supper?" Patty asked.

"No," Mother said. "Not this one. I'm going to take it over to Mrs. Adams. She's been sick in bed for several days. I thought it would be nice if I fixed something hot for the family. Would you like to come with me when I take it to her?"

"Oh, that would be fun," Patty told her mother.

A little later Mother took the hot dish out of the oven. She put a cover over it and started down the street. Patty skipped along beside her. Soon they came to the house where Mrs. Adams lived with her husband and three children.

21

Mrs. Adams was glad to see Mother. The children were glad to see Patty.

"You children can go out and play while I visit with Mrs. Adams," Mother said. "I'll call you when it's time for us to leave."

When Mr. Adams came home from work, Patty thought Mother must have forgotten all about calling them. But when she went inside the house she knew that wasn't true. Mother had been too busy to call. She had washed the dirty dishes that filled the sink. She had set the table for supper. It even looked as though she had mopped the kitchen floor.

"Mother, you said you were going to take Mrs. Adams a hot dish. You did lots more than that. You washed the dishes. You set the table. Even the floor looked clean. Did you wash it?"

"Yes, I did. But that's the way it should be. You know, when Jacob sent his sons into Egypt to buy corn, he sent double the money they needed. Then he added other gifts. And he told them to take a little honey, too. The extra things I did for Mrs. Adams today were just a little honey, dear.

"And best of all, I knew when I did these things for Mrs. Adams I was really doing them for the Lord Jesus."

Something to Think About: Do you think Mrs. Adams was glad that Patty's mother had come to see her? Why? What was the "little honey"? Suppose you were asked to pick up your toys. How could you add a "little honey" to what you do? When you wipe the dishes can you add a "little honey," too? How? Do you know anyone who needs your help as Mrs. Adams needed Patty's mother's help?

Bible Verse: "Whatsoever ye do to the least of these my brethren you do it unto me" (Matthew 25:40).

Prayer: Dear Lord Jesus, we thank You for showing us how to love people. Help us to go out of our way to be kind and loving to those who need our help. Help us to add a bit of honey, too. In Your dear Name. Amen.

How to Pack for Camp

Mary Jane was very, very excited. She was getting ready to go to Bible camp — and Mother had said she could pack her suitcase all by herself. Now she was ready to start. She put the suitcase on the bed and opened it. Then she went to the closet for her clothes.

But when she came back, she had a big surprise waiting for her. Sitting right in the middle of the suitcase was her little cocker spaniel puppy, Pogo.

She wondered how he had been able to get into the suitcase. She guessed he must have jumped onto a stool, onto the bed, then into the suitcase.

She tried to pick him up but he just cuddled down into a corner of the suitcase. He didn't want to move. Mary Jane laughed and laughed.

"You know you can't go with me," she said, though she was glad because he wanted to. "I'm going to Bible camp and the people who run the camp don't let little puppies come to camp." Once again she tried to pick him up. But Pogo made himself real heavy and snuggled closer into the suitcase corner.

"Mother!" Mary Jane called. "Come here. I want to show you something."

Mother came to see what Mary Jane wanted.

"Pogo thinks he should go to Bible camp with me," Mary Jane told her mother. "He crawled into the suitcase when I went into the closet and now he doesn't want to move. I wish I could take him with me."

Mother put her arm around Mary Jane's shoulder.

"I wish you could, too. But Pogo wouldn't be very welcome, I'm afraid. No — he's one thing you can't pack to take with you." She stopped and Mary Jane could see she was thinking about something else. "But, there are other things you can't pack either, things I hope you *will* take with you to camp."

"What do you mean?" Mary Jane wanted to know.

"Well," Mother said, "you can't pack good manners, can you? Nor can you pack a week of smiles, kindness, and love for others, can you?"

"I guess not," Mary Jane answered.

"They are things that prove you live in a Christian home," Mother told her. "Now back to your packing. I'll take Pogo . . . you pack your clothes. Just be sure you don't forget the things you can't pack. Okay?"

"Okay," Mary Jane answered. "They're just as important as my clothes, aren't they?"

Something to Think About: The early disciples had been told by the enemies of Jesus that they must not speak about Him. But the disciples said they couldn't stop talking about Him. He had changed their lives, so everything they said and did was proof that they had been with Him. How is their experience like Mary Jane's? Are there times when children forget to show that they have been brought up in a Christian home? How do you think Mary Jane should act at camp? How should she treat her counselors? Her roommates? Why is it important that boys and girls remember these things?

Bible Verse: "We can not but speak of the things which we have seen and heard" (Acts 4:20).

Prayer: Dear Father in heaven, like Mary Jane we sometimes leave home, too. We go to Bible camp. We go to school. We go to visit our relatives. Help us so that wherever we are we might prove that we know and love You. Watch over us this day. In Jesus' Name. Amen.

Tit for Tat

Perry and Gail were traveling through the mountains with their parents. Whenever they came to a spot that was especially pretty, Dad would stop the car. He'd park it alongside the road and they would all get out for a better look at the mountains.

It was at one of these stopping places that Perry and Gail learned that mountains can talk.

As they stood looking into the distance, Dad put his hand on Perry's shoulder.

"I wonder if we could hear our echo here?" he asked.

"What's an echo?" Perry asked.

"I'll show you," Dad said. He cupped his hands over his mouth. "Hi, there!" he shouted to the mountain across from them.

In no time at all a voice bounced right back. It said, "Hi, there!" It had a hollow sound, yet Perry and Gail could tell that it belonged to Father.

"How come?" Perry wanted to know.

"Well, I'm not sure I can explain it. I guess you'd say the sound waves made by my voice are bounced back to us."

"Would my voice bounce back, too?" Perry wanted to know.

"I think so," Dad said. "Try it."

Perry cupped his hands around his mouth as Dad had done. Then he shouted. "Hi, Perry!"

He waited. Sure enough. A voice shouted back, "Hi, Perry."

Perry lowered his voice and growled, "Hi, kid."

The voice growled, "Hi, kid."

"Think you're a tough guy, do you?" he asked gruffly.

The voice answered just as gruffly. "Think you're a tough guy, do you?"

Gail grabbed Perry's arm.

"It's my turn now," she said.

"Okay, you try it," Perry told her.

Gail cupped her hands over her mouth. Very sweetly she called, "Hi, Gail, I think you are a nice girl." Perry laughed. Dad and Mother smiled as they nudged each other. They waited.

The voice came back just as sweet as Gail's. "Hi, Gail, I think you are a nice girl."

"Say," Dad began excitedly. "We've got a lesson here. Did you notice that each of us got back exactly what he said? That's the way it is in life, too. If you are growly and mean, others are apt to be growly and mean to you. Be sweet and kind and you'll find you are treated that way, too."

"That's right!" Mother shouted.

Perry, Gail, and Dad jumped. Mother had taken them by surprise. They began to laugh. Here's why. In no time at all the words, "That's right!" came back just as she had said them.

Something to Think About: How should we treat other people? Why? Can you think of times when you forgot to treat someone as you would like to be treated? How can you remember this lesson?

Bible Verse: "And as ye would that men should do to you, do ye also to them likewise" (Luke 6:31).

Prayer: Dear Lord, we know that we are supposed to treat people as we would like to be treated. Help us to speak kindly about others. Help us to pray for others. Help us to love our enemies. Be with the leaders of our land. Guide them in all that they do. Keep reminding us to do good, not evil. In Jesus' Name. Amen.

God's Little Lamp

Because Mother and Dad had gone to a distant city on business, Aunt Jane had come to spend the night with Randy.

Now it was time for bed. Randy took his bath. Then he decided to surprise Aunt Jane, so he put on the pajamas she had given him for Christmas.

Aunt Jane was very pleased.

"How about a story?" she asked. Aunt Jane was a very good storyteller.

"Two?" Randy came back.

And two it was.

"Now your prayer," Aunt Jane said when she had finished telling the stories.

Randy knelt beside his bed and began to pray,

> "Jesus, tender shepherd, hear me
> Bless Thy little lamb tonight.
> Through the darkness be Thou near me
> Keep me safe 'til morning light.
>
> "All this day Thy hand has led me
> And I thank Thee for Thy care . . .
> Thou hast warmed me, clothed me, fed me.
> Listen to my evening prayer.
>
> "Let my sins be all forgiven
> Bless the friends I love so well —
> Take us all at last to heaven
> Happy there with Thee to dwell."

Aunt Jane was smiling when he was through. Randy wondered why. Then she told him.

"Randy, when I was a little girl, I prayed that very same prayer. But for years I prayed it a wee bit differently. When Mother taught it to me, I thought she said, 'Bless Thy little *lamp* tonight.' You see, I had a small kerosene lamp in my bedroom. I loved the lamp very much. So, it seemed quite all right to ask God to bless it.

27

"One night Mother realized I was saying *lamp* not *lamb*. She told me I should say lamb, because I was God's little lamb.

"But when I grew older, I came to believe my prayer wasn't too wrong at that."

"How come?" Randy asked.

"Well," Aunt Jane answered. "All who love Jesus are meant to be lamps for Him. So He needs to bless His lamps, too. See?"

Randy nodded. And, sometimes in the nights that followed, he would pray, "Bless Thy little lamp tonight." When he did, he always remembered what Aunt Jane had told him.

Something to Think About: Do you pray this nighttime prayer when you go to bed? If you don't, you might ask Mother to help you learn it. If Jesus is a Shepherd, who are His lambs? If Jesus is the Light of the world, how can we be His lamps? Where should our light shine?

Bible Verse: "Ye are the light of the world. . . . Let your light so shine before men, that they may see your good works and glorify your Father which is in heaven" (Matthew 5:14-16).

Prayer: Dear Lord Jesus, we thank You for caring for us as a shepherd does for his sheep. We thank You for giving Your light so we can shine as lamps for You. Help us to give a bright light wherever we go. In Thy Name. Amen.

God, Our Help

Ronnie Koleman had been crippled since he was a little boy. Polio had crippled him. In the years that followed his attack, Ronnie had several operations on his legs. Now he could walk. But he still had to wear a brace on his right leg.

And because he was growing, he had to go back to the brace shop to be refitted when he needed a new brace. A brace that didn't fit would rub his leg and make it hurt. So when he outgrew one, his folks bought him another.

Ronnie was so used to the brace he never thought much about it anymore. He played with his friends. He went for walks with his Dad. He did ever so many things he could not have done if he didn't wear a brace.

One day when Ronnie and his mother were in the brace shop, a woman came in with a small six-month-old baby. The baby had braces on both his feet. Mother, who was always friendly, began to talk to the lady. The lady told her the baby's feet were turned in the wrong direction when he was born. By wearing braces that were changed every few months, the baby's feet were being straightened.

"Isn't it wonderful," Mother said to the lady, "that doctors have discovered how to do these things? Wonderful, too, that braces come in all sizes."

"That's right," an old man who sat near by joined in the conversation. "I'm glad they make braces in my size. If I didn't wear one on my back, I wouldn't be much good. Now I can take care of my garden. I can go to the mailbox to get my mail. I can sit down at a table to eat. I'm thankful for my brace. It's never failed me once."

"*Never failed. . . .*" These words made Ronnie think about God. God has said He will never fail us, either. And He makes this promise to all sizes of people, too.

Something to Think About: Would a brace help a person who did not put it on? What does this teach you about your life and God? If you don't ask Him to come into your heart, can you expect Him to help you?

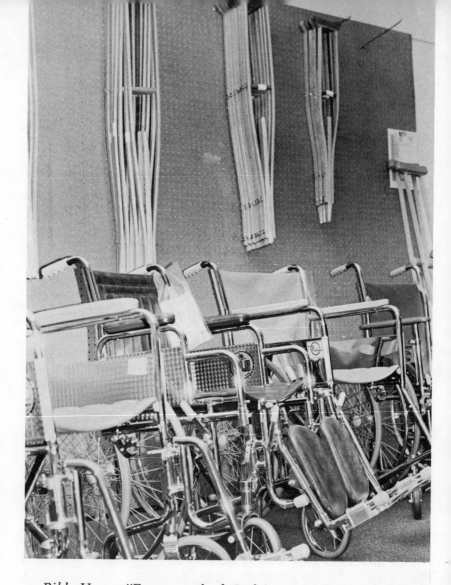

Bible Verse: "Every word of God is pure. He is a shield to them that put their trust in him" (Proverbs 30:5).

Prayer: Dear Lord, we praise You for your love and care. Thank You for giving us a good night's sleep. Thank You for school and home. Thank you for our church. Thank You for promising never to fail us. Help us always to trust You no matter how big or how old we are. In Jesus' Name. Amen.

The Seeing Eye Dog

Jan and Don were visiting their Uncle Norris in the capital city of their state. One day when they were out walking with Uncle Norris they saw a blind woman who was trying to get used to her seeing-eye dog. She was having trouble.

She seemed afraid to trust him to show her where to go. A couple of times she almost stumbled. And when she came to the street crossing, she stopped. The dog stepped into the street. But the woman held back. Just then a man who stood near by hurried to her side. Jan and Don wondered what he would do.

"He is her trainer," Uncle Norris told the children. "Listen to what he says to her."

The children stepped closer so they could hear what the man said.

"You can trust the dog," the trainer told the blind woman. "Just walk a little closer to him and he will show you where to go."

Something to Think About: Are you ever afraid? If you are this is a lesson for you, because you have a Friend you can trust, too. Don't pull away from Him; step closer and He will show you where to go.

Bible Verse: "Draw near to God and He will draw near to you" (James 4:8).

Prayer: Dear God, You are our heavenly Father. You know all about us. You know there are times when we don't know where to go. We lose our way. We are afraid. Be near us this day and show us where to go. In Jesus' Name. Amen.

The Way to Treat Sin

Sandra was visiting her Aunt Margaret. Sandra liked to visit her Aunt Margaret. Her apartment was always so nice and clean. Sandra liked the lovely records Aunt Margaret played on her record player. She liked to page through the bright-colored magazines that lay in a neat row on Aunt Margaret's coffee table.

Best of all, Sandra liked Aunt Margaret's candy bowl.

Sandra sat looking through a magazine now. But her mind wasn't on the magazine. It was on the candy bowl. After a while she put the magazine aside and stepped over to the candy bowl. She took off its lid and looked inside.

There were bright, striped peppermints in the bowl. Fat, foil-wrapped chocolates snuggled against cellophane-covered caramels. Sandra smacked her lips.

"Aunt Margaret," she called. "May I have a piece of candy?"

"Of course," Aunt Margaret called back from the kitchen where she and Mother were visiting while Aunt Margaret prepared supper.

Sandra dipped her hand into the candy bowl. She wasn't sure which kind she should take. She liked caramels. And she liked fat, foil-wrapped chocolates. She liked peppermints, too. She decided a chocolate would be best. As she unwrapped its foil covering, her mother put her head through the door and warned,

"Just one, Sandra. Supper will be ready soon. Aunt Margaret said it would only take a few minutes more. And I don't want you to spoil your appetite, you know."

"Okay," Sandra answered.

She slipped the cone-shaped chocolate into her mouth. It was smooth and yummy-chocolate good. She let it lie on her tongue and melt so it would last a long time. But it disappeared sooner than she liked. *Just one,* Mother had said. It had seemed so easy to say "Okay" before she ate the candy. Now it seemed she just had to have another piece to satisfy her candy hunger. She looked at the candy dish. She touched the cover — but she didn't lift the lid.

A few minutes later she climbed up on a chair beside her

mother. "Well," Mother said, "I thought you were looking at the magazine Aunt Margaret gave you. You aren't through with it already, are you?"

Sandra shook her head. She leaned over and whispered to her mother. "I'd rather be in here with you and Aunt Margaret," she said. "Besides, the candy dish is in there."

Mother laughed. She pinched Sandra's cheek teasingly. "Out of sight, out of mind, is that it?" she asked.

Sandra wasn't sure what that meant — but she guessed it had something to do with the candy dish.

Something to Think About: Why did Sandra leave the living room and go into the kitchen? Do you think she was wise? Why? This is a good lesson to remember when you are tempted in any way. If there are friends who want you to do what is wrong, leave them. Go away from them. When Satan tells you to sin, run away from him.

Bible Verse: "Flee (run away from) temptation and follow after the things that are good" (I Timothy 6:11).

Prayer: Dear Heavenly Father, we thank You for this day. We thank You for food and clothes, for sunshine and rain. We thank You for this lesson about Sandra. Help us to remember to run away from temptation, too. In Jesus' Name. Amen.

The Best Medicine

Joe and Anne were tired of riding. It seemed they had been on the road for days and days. Really it had only been a few hours. But it seemed a long time.

"Why don't you play some games?" Mother asked.

"We've played all the games we know," Joe told his mother.

Mother wrinkled her forehead as she always did when she was thinking. "Let me see . . ." she said, and Joe and Anne knew she was trying to think of something for them to do.

"Here's an idea," she said suddenly. "Let's try to find sign boards that have interesting messages on them. As soon as you see one, read it. Then I'll write it on a piece of paper. Whoever has found the most at the end of the hour will get a special treat." Joe and Anne thought this would be fun. They leaned forward in their seats and began to watch the signs along the highway.

A short time later Joe found a sign that said, "Go to church on Sunday" and another that read, "Honesty pays." Sometimes the messages were part of a big sign. Sometimes they were on buildings. Sometimes they stood all alone by the side of the road like the one that said, "There's nothing like money in the bank."

It was Anne who found a sign on a church bulletin board. She hoped Joe wouldn't see it. She squinted her eyes to see better. Then as they approached the sign, she began to read, "This church is open for pr . . . a . . . yer . . ." It was hard to make out the rest because the sign stood in the shade of a tree, but she kept on, *"and medication!"* She shouted the last two words excitedly.

Dad, who was driving the car, began to laugh. Mother laughed, too.

"Dope," Joe kidded teasingly. "That's not medication, that's meditation."

"Well, what's the difference?" Anne wanted to know.

It was mother who explained that meditation means worship and thinking about God. Medication is medicine.

"Well, maybe Anne isn't too wrong at that," Dad said. "Surely

the church is good medicine. Doesn't the One it stands for cure sin? Doesn't He give peace to worried people? Doesn't He make people strong?"

"You are right," Mother said. Joe and Anne nodded. The whole family agreed church and what it teaches is the best medicine in the whole world.

Something to Think About: Why is the Gospel of Jesus Christ good medicine? What sickness does it cure? How can we take this medicine? Is it important that we take it regularly? Will it make any difference if we skip a few doses? Why?

Bible Verse: "Who forgiveth your sins and heals your diseases" (Psalm 103:3).

Prayer: Dear Lord, our Heavenly Father, we worship and love You with all our hearts. We know that You can heal our sins. You can make us glad when we are sad. You can cure our angry tempers. You can help us when we are worried or fearful. We thank You that we have churches where we can worship You. Bless and keep us this day. In Jesus' Name. Amen.

See-Saw

Lynn and Lowell were vacationing with their parents at a northern Minnesota cottage. The cottage belonged to Mother's uncle.

One day Mother's uncle visited the cottage where they were staying. He found Lynn and Lowell trying to saw some logs. They needed wood for the fireplace.

But they weren't doing very well. When Lowell pulled the saw in his direction, Lynn pushed it toward him too fast. Lowell did the same thing when Lynn pulled it toward her. Sometimes they forgot and both of them pulled the saw at the same time.

"Wait a minute," Uncle said as he walked over to the wooden horse that held the log. "You've got to learn to work together. Come, John," he called to the children's father. "Let's show these kids how to saw wood the right way."

Dad walked over to the saw and picked up one end of it. Uncle took the other. Back and forth, back and forth. How easily and evenly the saw chewed its way through the log. When Uncle pulled the saw, Dad let it ride back lightly. He kept it right in place as Uncle pulled toward him. When Dad pulled the saw, Uncle did the same thing.

"Cooperation, that's all," Uncle told the children. "It's that way with a family, too. When you do your part and the other fellow does his, your work will always go smoothly. If both of you pull in opposite directions, you'll have trouble."

That evening after dinner the children had a chance to prove that cooperation works in washing dishes as well as in sawing wood. Usually they both wanted to dry the dishes. Neither wanted to wash them. Now they decided they'd take turns.

"Remember Uncle said it's cooperation that counts," Lowell told Lynn as he merrily sloshed his hands around in the soapy water.

Bible Verse: "Do to others as you would want them to do to you" (Luke 6:31).

Something to Think About: Why is this a good verse to think about? What does "cooperation" mean? If you were Mother,

36

what would you want your children to do for you? If Mother were you, what would she want done for her? Why do you suppose the family that works together, that prays together, and that attends church together is the most happy?

Prayer: Dear Father in heaven, forgive me. So often I want to do things my own way. Thank You for the lesson about the saw. Help us as a family to work together to please You. Keep us in Thy love so we can always do our best work wherever we are. In Jesus' Name. Amen.

37

What Pruning Means

"Mother!" Nancy called to her mother one beautiful day in May. "Where are you?"

"In the front yard," Mother called back.

Nancy came running.

But when she saw what Mother was doing, she stopped short. Her mouth dropped open.

"Oh, no, don't do that," she begged.

Mother laughed. Nancy couldn't understand why. She didn't think what Mother was doing was funny. Mother was picking all the small buds off the peony plants. On each stalk she left only one bud. And Nancy didn't like that.

"I suppose you think I am hurting the peonies," Mother said. "Well, aren't you?" Nancy wanted to know.

"No, I'm helping them. If all the buds were left on the stalks, none of them would grow very large. The plant would have to share food and strength with all of them. By pinching all but one, I let the plant give all its strength to the main blossom."

Nancy shook her head. She still didn't believe what her mother was doing was right.

"I'll tell you what I'll do," Mother said, "I'll leave all the buds on a few plants just to see what happens."

In a week or so the peonies were in bloom. And this is what Nancy discovered. Mother was right! The biggest blossoms were on the plants where she had pinched off the small buds.

When Mother saw that Nancy understood, she told her that was the way she wanted her to grow. When she said, "No!" "Now, don't be cross!" or "Watch that tongue!" she was really pinching buds that shouldn't grow. She wanted Nancy to become a beautiful blossom for Christ.

Something to Think About: This pinching back of buds is called pruning. Sometimes even branches of trees are cut away so the tree can grow as it should. Do you think children need to be "pruned" by their parents? Can they help prune each other? How? Would you like to grow up without ever being corrected? Why not?

Bible Verse: "He that listens to correction is wise" (Proverbs 15:5).

Prayer: Dear Lord Jesus, we know that we sometimes grow in a direction that is wrong. We let buds develop in our lives that shouldn't be there. Thank You for parents who care how we grow. We want You to help prune us, too. Keep us sweet and kind. Help us to be honest with others. Forgive us for the times we talk back and fail to do what we know is right. In Jesus' Name. Amen.

The Place to Start

Mike and Jerry braked their bikes to a sudden halt.

"Detour!" Mike exclaimed disappointedly.

Mike and Jerry, neighbor boys, had huffed and puffed their way over the crest of the hill on the way to the lake. They expected to find clear sailing on the other side. Instead, men and machines blocked the road at the bottom of the hill. And, a big sign marked the place where they worked.

"Come, let's see what the sign says," Jerry said as he eased his bike to glide down the hill.

When they came to the sign, Mike read,

"CAUTION — ROAD UNDER. . . ." *That's funny,* he thought. Someone had changed the sign! The first part of the word "construction" had been painted over. Someone had changed the word to "destruction." Now the sign said, "CAUTION — ROAD UNDER DESTRUCTION."

Now, both boys knew that construction means to build; destruction means to tear apart.

"Well, isn't that true?" Jerry shouted to Mike, trying to make himself heard above the noise of drills and hammers that were breaking up the road.

"I guess so," Mike answered. "They've got to get rid of the old road before they can build a new one."

What the boys learned about road building is true about life, too. If you want to build a good habit, you have to destroy the old one first. And, if you want to make a wrong thing right, you have to go clear to the bottom of it, to admit it and ask God to remove it. Only then do we have a right to ask God to make us new and whole again.

Something to Think About: Are there things in your life you ought to ask God to forgive? Are there stains that need to be wiped away? Is there an old road that needs to be destroyed? Who can help you do this? When is the best time to begin? Why?

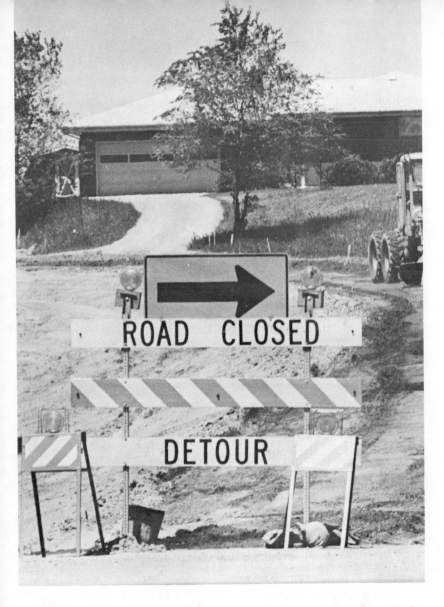

Bible Verse: "Create in me a new heart, O Lord" (Psalm 51:7).

Prayer: Dear Lord, we thank You that You are a life builder. We know You know all about us and can see things what ought to be destroyed in our life. Show us the mistakes we make. Forgive them, too. We pray in Jesus' Name. Amen.

No Fooling

Joel loved birds and animals. And because he did, they liked him, too. He'd made friends with the wild rabbit who had her nest of young bunnies under one of Dad's pine shrubs. A big, bushy-tailed squirrel often crept near to beg Joel for food. He'd even taught a robin he called "Robin Red" to eat out of his hand.

One day Joel decided he was going to have some fun. He took some of his parakeet's food in his hand. Then he went outside and called his friend, Robin Red.

He whistled his special call to her. Sure enough, when Robin Red heard Joel, she flew to him. She perched herself on his wrist and waited for him to open his hand so she could eat the food he had for her.

Slowly, ever so slowly, Joel began to straighten his fingers. But just as Robin Red got ready to reach for the food, Joel snapped his hand shut.

Robin Red cocked her head to one side, a puzzled expression in her beady eyes.

This is fun, Joel thought. He tried again — opening his hand, then closing it when his feathered friend stretched her neck to pick up the food.

Joel fooled Robin Red several times. *Just once more,* he told himself. But before he could open his hand, Robin Red flew away. Joel whistled to her. She did not come. He called softly, "Come, Reddy, come and I'll give you some food." But no matter how much he coaxed, Robin Red would have nothing to do with him. And no wonder! Joel had fooled her just once too often.

Something to Think About: Did you know some people treat Jesus in the same way Joel treated Robin Red? They decide they are going to open their hearts to Him, but when the time comes, they turn away from Him. They say they will wait until a later day. They do this over and over again. When they grow older, they find they don't even want to think about Jesus. They don't even hear when He knocks at their heart door and asks

to come in. The Bible says such people have "hardened their hearts" to Him. That's why it is so important that you learn about Jesus when you are young. That's why you should let Him come into your heart now.

Bible Verse: "Behold I stand at the door and knock" (Revelation 3:20).

Prayer: Dear Lord Jesus, come into our hearts right now. "Come in today, come in to stay, Come into our hearts, Lord Jesus." We thank You that You love us and want to live in our hearts. We thank You for giving Your life for us. Help us each day to treat those we meet with the same kind of love You have showed to us. In Your Name. Amen.

God Understands

Dianne opened her eyes slowly. She looked around the room. It was a room she had never seen before. *Where am I?* she asked herself.

Just then she felt a smooth hand on her forehead. It was Mother's hand. She would know it anywhere. She turned her head. Mother smiled down at her.

"Where am I?" Dianne asked.

"You are in the hospital," Mother told her. "You've been a very, very sick girl. But you are better now."

"How did I get here?" Dianne wanted to know.

"You came in an ambulance," Mother said. "But you didn't come alone. Dr. McFarlane rode with you — and so did I. You've been asleep for several days."

Dianne tried to sit up. Ever so gently, Mother pushed her back against the pillow.

"Not yet, dear. You'll have to lie still a while longer."

Dianne reached up and took her Mother's hand.

"I'm glad you are here," Dianne told Mother as she squeezed her hand.

"I'm glad, too. And you aren't to worry. I am going to stay with you as long as you need me. You see, when Mother was a little girl, she was sick as you are now. She understands exactly how you feel."

Something to Think About: Mother was very sorry Dianne was ill. Because she had had the same sickness when she was a child, she understood exactly how Dianne felt. God has the same love for His children as parents do. Do you think He understood how Dianne felt? This is something to remember when you are sick. God has said He will never leave or forsake us.

Bible Verse: "As a father (or mother) pitieth his children so the Lord pitieth them that love him" (Psalm 103:13).

Prayer: Dear Lord Jesus, we thank You for watching over us as You do. We thank You for loving us no matter what we do. We thank You for understanding when we are sick, for giving us parents who love us, too. In Jesus' Name. Amen.

Knots That Can't Be Untied

John and Paul Baxter liked to play in the woods near their home. They liked to watch the birds fly among the branches. They liked to hear the bluejays scold. They liked when the leaves sang in the cool spring breeze. They liked to stand beside the tall pines that stretched long, bushy arms toward the sky. Sometimes it seemed they almost reached the sky. Another reason the boys liked the woods was because they were always finding something there that they had never seen before.

That's the way it was the day they discovered the tree that looked as if a knot had been tied in it. The knot was about half way up the tree. The boys looked at it. They walked around it. *How could a tree grow that way?* the boys wondered. The trunk was at least four inches through the middle. Surely no one could have tied a knot in a tree that was so big.

When Dad came home from work, Paul and John showed him the tree.

"It's a knot, all right," Mr. Baxter told his sons. "But it must have been tied a long, long time ago. I think it was tied when the tree was a tiny sapling." He ran his long fingers over the pattern of the knot as he spoke.

"Maybe this is the way it happened," he said. "Long ago some boy may have played in these woods just as you do now. When he felt the young sapling, he discovered that it could be bent very easily. Twisting it under and around itself, he tied a knot in it."

Mr. Baxter examined the tree again. Then he turned back to the boys.

"Do you think you could untie that knot?"

"You kidding?" Paul said. "It's grown together that way now. No one could ever untie the knot."

"That's what I wanted you to say," the boys' father said. "It's that way with young fellows like you, too. There's an old truth that says, 'As a twig is bent. . . .' which means as boys are bent, so the man will grow. The way you start out in life, the habits you make when you are young, will determine the kind

of person you will be when you grow up. Knots tied in young boys' lives are just as hard to untie as this tree knot."

Something to Think About: Why do you think Mother and Dad want you to learn to obey when you are young? How are habits like knots in a tree? Can you name some habits that should be shunned? When should habit knots be untied? Why couldn't the boys untie the tree knot?

Bible Verse: "Train up a child in the way he should go, and when he is old he will not depart from it" (Proverbs 22:6).

Prayer: Dear Lord, we are glad that You can keep our lives free from ugly knots. We thank You for Sunday school teachers, for parents and for pastors who teach us how to live — so we won't have any knots in our minds and souls. Help us to choose wisely the things we do. May we always be pleasing to You. In Jesus' dear Name. Amen.

The Way You Look at Things

Susie looked up from her dinner plate.

"Mom," she began, "why is Paula Rogers such a mean kid?"

"I've never thought of her as being mean," Mother answered.

"Well, she is."

"What makes you say that?"

"You just ought to hear the way she talks."

"How does she talk?" Mother asked.

"Well, it happened this way," Susie explained. "Just before we went into Sunday school, I met Paula in the hall. She was all dressed up, of course, for Sunday, you know. She looked all right except for one thing. So, I said —

" 'Paula, where in the world did you get that funny hat?' "

"Oh, no!" Mother exclaimed.

"That's all I said," Susie hurried to explain. "Then do you know what she did? She made a face at me and said, real mean like —

" 'Shut up!' Isn't that awful?"

Something to Think About: Susie saw Mother give Daddy a strange look. Then she turned back to Susie. "Which was worse? For you to tell her she had a funny hat or for her to get angry with you?"

Mother's question was a good one. Was Susie kind when she made fun of Paula's hat?

The sad thing about it all was that Susie didn't realize she had done anything wrong.

Jesus talked a great deal about people who criticize and find fault with others. He called this "throwing stones." He said such persons should get rid of the wrong in their own lives before they threw stones at someone else.

Bible Verse: "He who is without sin, let him cast the first stone" (John 8:7).

Prayer: Dear Lord Jesus, thank You for this day. Thank You for health and home and love. Help us to see the wrong we do. And keep us from *throwing stones* at others. Help us to be kind in all we do and say. In Jesus' Name. Amen.

"Jimmy Hit Me"

Sandy came into the house crying as if her heart would break.

Mother sat down and took Sandy in her lap. She hugged her close and wiped the tears that spilled down her cheeks.

"Now, now," Mother comforted, smoothing Sandy's hair away from her eyes. "It can't be as bad as all that. Tell me what happened."

Sandy sobbed some more. Mother waited.

"Can you tell me now?" Mother asked.

"Jimmy hit me!" Sandy blurted. Jimmy was the little neighbor boy who often played with Sandy. "We were playing in the sand box and he hit me."

"What were you quarreling about?" Mother asked.

"We decided the sand box was a big farm. But Jimmy wasn't fair. He said he should have a bigger part of it just because he's a couple years older. And he hit me!" The tears began to fall again.

"And what did you do? Did you hit him back?"

"No," Sandy said as she sat up in Mother's lap, clenching her teeth in anger. "I hit him first."

Something to Think About: Do you feel sorry for Sandy? Why? Or why not?

This story proves there are always two sides to a quarrel. If Sandy hadn't hit Jimmy, he may never have hit her. Sometimes our selfishness makes enemies. Perhaps Jimmy had a special reason for wanting the bigger part of the sand box. Sandy should have talked about it instead of becoming angry. Suppose Jimmy would have been angry anyway. What would you have done if you had been Sandy?

Bible Verse: "Thou shalt love thy neighbor as thyself" (Leviticus 19:18).

"He that is slow to anger is better than the mighty; and he that ruleth (can control) his spirit than he that taketh a city" (Proverbs 16:32).

Prayer: Dear Lord, You know how easy it is for us to get angry when we don't get our way. You have taught us that this is wrong. Forgive us for the times when we have forgotten Your teaching. Keep us in Thy love this day. Help us by our actions to prove that we love You. In Jesus' Name. Amen.

Who Peeked?

Church is the place where men and women, boys and girls worship God.

Donny knew this was true. He had gone to church with his parents almost as long as he could remember.

He had been taught to sit quietly. He had been taught to follow the songs he knew. And Dad and Mother had taught him to close his eyes and fold his hands when the pastor or anyone else prayed.

One Sunday morning Donny sat right next to a boy who was new in church. Donny had met him in his Sunday school class. When he sat down, Donny smiled, showing him he was glad he was in church. He shared his song book with the new boy, too.

But imagine's Dad's surprise when, after the pastor had prayed, Donny nudged him to show that he wanted to tell him something. Dad leaned over to hear what Donny had to say.

"Dad," Donny whispered, "Johnny peeked!"

Something to Think About: How do you suppose Donny knew that Johnny peeked? No doubt he peeked, too. He hadn't kept his eyes closed during prayer. If he had, he would not have seen that Johnny did not close his eyes. Isn't that just like us? We can see when someone else does wrong. We are quick to blame them. But we excuse ourselves when we do the same thing.

Bible Verse: "Search me, O God, and know my heart; try me and know my thoughts and see if there be any wicked way in me. Lead me in the way that is always right" (Psalm 139: 23, 24).

Prayer: Dear God, we know You have told us to examine our own hearts to see if there is any wicked thing in them. You can teach us to know when we sin. Help us not to expect more of others than we expect of ourselves. Forgive us for so often disobeying You. Forgive us for finding fault with others. Keep our tongues from speaking wrong. In Jesus' Name. Amen.

Knowing Who You Are

Uncle Jim had come to visit the Jackson family. Mary and Dave were always glad when Uncle Jim stopped by. Uncle Jim was fun. He was a captain in the army and he always had so many interesting stories to tell.

At supper Uncle Jim told a story that made Mary and Dave stop and think. Uncle Jim had just come from a big meeting of army men. His story happened there.

"You know," he said, "right in the middle of the meeting a man stood up. The chairman asked him what he wanted. This is what he said,

" 'I came here because I am an amnesic.' That means he had lost his memory and couldn't remember anything about himself. 'I have been a soldier. So I thought maybe some of you people would be able to help me. Does anyone here know who I am?' "

"Did anyone know?" Dave asked eagerly.

"No," Uncle Jim told him. "No one knew the man."

Something to Think About: To be lost to family and friends is certainly very sad. Not to know whether you are a banker, a farmer, or a teacher, whether you have a family or not must be very disturbing. But, there is something much worse. That would be not to know, not to be sure you belong to Jesus. The Bible says we can be sure. If we believe in our hearts and confess with our mouths that Jesus is the Christ we become a child of His. Then we will know that His Spirit lives in our lives. We are His children.

Bible Verse: "For I know in whom I have believed and am persuaded (sure) that he will keep me always" (II Timothy 1:12).

Prayer: Dear Jesus, thank You for making it possible for us to belong to You. Thank You for Your promise to take care of us always. Help us to show, by loving others, that we are Your children. Forgive our sins and guide us this day. In Jesus' Name. Amen.

Ask for Help

No matter how hard Jerry tried, he could not move the big branch that lay across the driveway.

"That mean old wind!" he grumbled as he tugged at the branch. Jerry was angry at the wind because it had broken off the branch of a nearby tree. He wanted to ride his tricycle in the driveway. But he couldn't ride it as long as the branch blocked his way.

He struggled some more. Finally he decided to give up. As he turned away from the branch, he almost stumbled into his father.

"Oh, excuse me," he said, surprised. "I didn't know you were watching me."

"Can't you move the branch?" his father asked.

"Nope," Jerry answered. "It won't budge."

"Have you tried everything you could think of?" Dad asked

"Sure, but nothing helps."

"I know something you didn't try," Jerry's father told him.

"What?" Jerry asked excitedly, because he really wanted the broken branch out of the way.

"You haven't tried me," Dad told him.

Something to Think About: This little story tells more than it seems to. Can you find its hidden meaning? It is this. God is like a father. And, as a father, He wants you to know that there will be branches in your life that you won't be able to move alone. They, too, block your way. A bad temper is this kind of branch. So are stubbornness and dishonesty. If you are wise, you will ask God to help you overcome these problems, to move the bad branches out of your way.

Bible Verse: "God is our refuge and strength, a very present help in time of trouble" (Psalm 46:1).

Prayer: Dear Lord, so often we forget that You have said You will help us when we call You. Forgive us. Teach us which branches should be moved in our lives. We need Your help every minute of every day. Be with us and near us always. In Jesus' Name. Amen.

"Dear God, I Love You"

Little Mary skipped out of the house and down the walk. It was Sunday morning and Mother and Dad, Charles, James and Mary were on their way to Sunday school. Mother and Dad walked together. Charles and James walked together. But Mary skipped on ahead of the rest.

The bright morning sun, the clean, fresh air and the green, green grass, everything, seemed to tell Mary that God loved her. She couldn't remember ever having felt so happy.

She wished there were some way she could tell God that she loved Him, too. Suddenly she stopped. She could tell Him, she thought. Right now. So, looking up into the sky she waved her white gloved hand and called,

"Dear God, I love You!"

Something to Think About: Some people would laugh at Mary because she stopped to talk to God. But Mother and Dad didn't. James and Charles didn't. Do you know why? They had been taught that God hears when people talk to Him. Mary was, as we say, "on speaking terms with God." She was used to talking to Him. She felt His nearness and wanted to show Him she loved Him. Do you love God so much that you stop to talk to Him anytime? Anywhere?

Bible Verse: "Delight thyself in the Lord and He shall give you the desires of your heart" (Psalm 37:4).

Prayer: Dear God in heaven, thank You for the sun that shines. Thank You for the green grass. Thank You for flowers and trees. Thank You for loving us every moment of every day. Thank You for our homes, for love, for our family and friends. Right now we praise Your holy Name because we love You, too. In Jesus' Name. Amen.

The "Quits Kids"

Breathlessly and like a small cyclone, Paul flung himself into the kitchen where Mother was busy with her work.

"My, my!" Mother said. "What are you so excited about?"

"It's something I want to ask you."

"Well?" Mother asked.

"Jim said there used to be a program on the radio where kids our age answered questions . . . all kinds of questions . . . about the moon . . . about music . . . about cars and airplanes."

"He's right," Mother said. "Did he tell you the name of the program?"

"That's what I wanted to ask you. He said it was called the 'Quits Kids.' I didn't believe him. So I said I'd ask you."

Paul thought his mother looked at him strangely almost as if she didn't hear him right.

"*Quits* Kids?" Mother asked.

"Hmmmhmmm."

Mother began to laugh. "*Quizz* Kids, Paul, not *Quits* Kids. "The 'Quits Kids' live here?"

Something to Think About: Do you know what the word *quit* means? Do you ever quit (stop doing) a job before it is really finished? What do you think Paul's mother meant when she said, "The 'Quits Kids' live here"?

In talking about our love for God, Jesus spoke about "staying true"; "holding fast" and "keeping faith," which mean just the opposite of quitting. There are people who begin to walk with Christ, then quit or grow tired of doing what is right. It was about such people Jesus spoke.

Bible Verse: "Let us not be weary of doing good for after a time we will be rewarded if we do not tire of our task" (Galatians 6:9).

Prayer: Dear Lord Jesus, we thank You that You did not tire and grow weary of the work You were sent to do. Thank You for forgiving our sin. Help us always to stay true to You. Help us, too, in our daily lives to finish what we are told to do. In Thy dear Name. Amen.

Grandfather's Lifesavers

Grandfather always sat near the front of the church. He wanted to be sure he didn't miss a single word of the minister's message.

One Sunday morning, right after the first song had been sung, he noticed a little boy pushing his way past the other people in the pew. The boy was edging toward him. Grandfather smiled. He knew who that boy was. It was Timmy Joe, his little grandson. Timmy often came to sit in the pew with Grandfather.

Grandfather moved over to make room for his grandson. After Timmy was seated, he pulled Grandfather toward him. Grandfather realized Timmy wanted to tell him something. He leaned toward the boy.

"Grandpa," Timmy whispered. "I came up to sit by you because I didn't want you to be lonesome. . . ." He took a deep breath, leaned closer and whispered still more softly, "Got any lifesavers?"

Something to Think About: Why did Timmy Joe want to sit by his grandfather? Was it really because he didn't want him to be lonesome? Or was he kind to his grandfather because he wanted to get something from him? He knew Grandfather usually had candy and that was what he wanted, wasn't it?

The Bible says this type of kindness is wrong. We should be kind to people even if they can't do anything for us.

Bible Verse: ". . . if you do good to them which do good to you, what thank have you? . . . But love your enemies and do good, and lend, hoping for nothing in return, and your reward shall be great" (Luke 6:33-35).

Prayer: Dear Lord Jesus, You did good to people who could not pay You back. You did good because You loved them and wanted to help them. Thank You for teaching us what real kindness means. Show us the way to be kind to others, too. In Your dear Name. Amen.

Counting the Cost

Dad had just brought Mother and the new baby home from the hospital.

Anne and Tommy were delighted.

"May we hold him?" they asked.

"Of course," Mother answered.

She let Tommy hold him first. Anne, who was younger, stood by his side. She kissed the baby's tiny, chubby fingers. All of a sudden she noticed a small plastic band on his wrist. She looked at it, turned it over, then puzzled, she asked,

"Aren't we going to take off his price tag?"

Mother and Dad laughed.

"Dope," Tommy teased. "Didn't you know he was free?"

"That's his name tag, dear," Mother explained. "The nurses put it on him so we'd be sure to get our own baby." Then she added, "But he wasn't all free — there was a hospital bill, the doctor's fee. . . ."

"And, don't forget your part," Dad told Mother.

"We don't count that!" Mother answered. "He's worth everything he cost. Don't you think so, children?"

Both Tommy and Anne nodded, though they weren't quite sure they knew what Mother meant.

Something to Think About: Being born into God's family is something like being born into a human family. We say salvation is free. Yet it cost God something. What did it cost God? And it cost Jesus something. What did it cost Him? Have you thanked Him for giving His life for you?

Bible Verse: "For God so loved the world that he gave his only begotten Son, that whosoever believeth on him should not perish but have everlasting life" (John 3:16).

Prayer: Dear Heavenly Father, You are a wise, all-knowing God. You knew that we could not be saved unless You sent Your Son to earth to die for us. Thank You for sending Him to be our Saviour. Help us to tell others what it cost Him to reclaim us. In His blessed Name. Amen.

A Gift of Our Own

Jim was Susan's city cousin. For months she had looked forward to his visit. *What fun we will have,* she thought. She would show Jim the new baby kittens. They would sail boats in the meadow brook. And best of all, they would ride Candy, Susan's blond Shetland pony. "We'll take turns," Susan told her mother.

Finally the day came when Jim arrived by train. But, for several days after his arrival, he didn't see the baby kittens; he didn't sail boats in the meadow brook. Nor did he ride Candy, Susan's blond Shetland pony.

Here is why. Susan and Jim were kept indoors by a long, hard summer rain.

"What can we do?" Susan moaned.

"You could color your new picture books," Mother suggested.

"Let's!" Jim almost shouted the words. It didn't take Susan long to understand why. Jim was a real artist when it came to coloring picture books.

When Susan saw his pictures, she stopped coloring. She could never get hers as nice as he got his. Never. Little by little jealousy began to creep into Susan's heart. It just wasn't fair that he could color so well, she told herself.

Mother was wise. When she learned that Susan was jealous of Jim, she took her aside for one of those "private" talks mothers have with their children.

"Can Jim play the piano?" Mother asked.

"No, I don't think so," Susan answered.

"But you can." Mother told her. Then she asked another question. "Can Jim bake cookies?"

"No. . . ."

"Do you remember how much he liked the cookies you baked for him?"

Susan nodded. Mother went on,

"Each of us can do something real well. We aren't all made alike. God gave Jim his drawing talent. He gave you your love for music. Be glad you can do what you can do. Be glad Jim can do what he can do."

"But I want to color as good pictures as he does."

"Why don't you ask him to show you how?" Mother asked.

"That's an idea," Susan said as she skipped away to join her city cousin, Jim.

Something to Think About: Did you know no two snowflakes are exactly alike? Nor are the fingerprints of any two people alike. God made each of us as we are. Some people can sing. Some can draw. Some make good teachers; others good preachers.

Jesus likened people to parts of the human body. He is the Head, He said. Each of us is a different part. Each has a special job to do for Him.

What talents or gifts has He given you? How can you use them for Him?

Bible Verse: "So we being many are one body in Christ, and every one members of another. Having gifts that differ according to what he has given us" (Romans 12:5, 6).

Prayer: Dear Lord, we thank You for Your love and care for us each day. You know what talents You have given us. Help us to understand what they are and be willing to develop them so we can serve You as You have planned. In Jesus' Name. Amen.

Open Your Hand

"Mother!" Paul called from the back yard where he and his friend, Richard, were playing. "Can you come here?"

Mother was busy washing dishes. But she wiped her hands on a towel and hurried to see what her son wanted.

"Look!" Paul pointed to the sand box where he and Richard had set up a play town. "Richard can't get his hand out of that bottle."

He was right! Richard's hand was caught inside a bottle. He pulled his fist this way; he pulled it that way, but it wouldn't come out through the neck of the bottle.

"Well," Mother said thoughtfully. "And how did you get your hand in the bottle?"

Before Richard had a chance to explain, Paul exclaimed, "Oh, that was easy, Mom. His hand was open and empty then."

Mother smiled. Once again she spoke to Richard.

"Have you tried opening your hand now?"

"Oh, I couldn't do that," Richard told her. "Then I'd lose my marbles."

Something to Think About: "What a foolish boy!" Is that what you are saying? Yet Richard is no more foolish than many people, some a great deal older than he. They want all the things that being a Christian offers — peace with God, happiness, forgiveness of sins, heaven — but they don't want to let go of sinful things in their lives.

These sinful things are like the marbles in Richard's hands. When people let go of them, they have an open hand to take the things God offers. Name the things a person must drop if he is going to be a happy Christian.

Bible Verse: "He that covereth his sins shall not prosper: but whosoever confesseth and forsaketh (drops) them shall be blessed" (Proverbs 28:13).

Prayer: Dear Lord, we know You came to the world to take away all our sins. Thank You for Your great love. Teach us which "sin marbles" we must drop. Help us to give up everything that displeases You. In Jesus' Name. Amen.

All of My Heart

Trudy and Don sat cross-legged on the kitchen floor. Trudy, who was the younger child, had just returned from a visit to her aunt. While she was gone, she had had a birthday. Besides gifts, folks had given her money. Now she was showing her brother the different coins she had received. The money lay in a little pile on the floor between them.

All of a sudden Trudy realized that she had all this money and Don had none. Because she loved her brother very much, she reached down and separated some of the coins from the pile.

"Here, you can have these," she told Don.

Don thanked her and began to examine the coins. Looking at them, Trudy realized she had more than he. She reached down again and shoved a few more coins toward her brother.

Perhaps it was because she loved him and had missed him so much while she was gone that made her do what she did next.

She looked at him lovingly. Then quickly, with a wide sweep of her hand, she pushed all of the money into his pile.

"There, you can have them all," she told him.

Something to Think About: What Trudy did that day is a good example of how we should show our love for God. There is a song that says, "What shall I give Thee, Master?" In one part we sing, "Not just a part, but all of my heart. . . ."

Some people give God only a part of their lives. They go to Sunday school or to church. On Sunday they say they love Him. But on Monday they forget all about Him. This isn't right. A Christian is a Christian all the time. He gives God not just a part but *all of his heart.*

Bible Verse: "Thou shalt love the Lord thy God with all thy heart, and with all thy soul and with all thy might" (Deuteronomy 6:5).

Prayer: Dear Jesus, thank You for this story about Trudy and how she showed her love for her brother. Help us to love You with all we have, too. May we say or do only the things that will please You this day. Forgive us our sins. In Jesus' Name. Amen.

A Man Is Remembered for His Work

Many years ago a boy named David Livingstone was born in faraway Scotland. Because his parents were poor, David went to work in a cotton factory when he was only ten years old.

But even though he had very little money, David managed to get an education. After many years of hard work and study, he became a doctor. But he didn't stay in Scotland to practice medicine. Somehow he heard about the many people in Africa who had never heard about Jesus Christ. Right then and there he decided he would tell them. He would be a preacher-doctor. He would go to Africa.

He did. And in his travels he went far inland, helping people who had never before seen a white man.

When he died, he was buried in Westminster Abbey, London, England, a place where people who have come to be known as great men are buried.

Now this is what you should remember. David had a brother. His name was John. When John and David were young, they used to talk about what they'd like to be when they grew older.

Later, unlike David, John became a businessman. He was a good one, too. When he died he left a great deal of money. David, however, died penniless. Yet it isn't John who is remembered today. Few people even know that he lived. It is David Livingstone whom the world has grown to love.

Something to Think About: Why is David Livingstone remembered today? Why is John forgotten? We could say that David Livingstone's work lives on. How? Where?

Everyone who works for Christ finds that his work lives on in the hearts of people he has won for the Lord.

If God calls you to serve Him, will you be willing to go wherever He wants you to go?

Bible Verse: "I heard the voice of the Lord saying, 'Whom shall I send and who will go for me?' Then said I, 'Here am I, send me'" (Isaiah 6:8).

Prayer: Dear Lord Jesus, we thank You for calling David Livingstone to work for You. We thank You for all the men and women who love and serve You. When we decide what we should do when we grow up, help us to listen for Your call. Keep our lives pure and clean for You. In Thy dear Name. Amen.

The Broken Moon

Dana loved to watch the big gold moon as it peeked over the edge of the world and climbed across the sky.

She was too small to understand that the moon really has no light of its own. She didn't know its light is just a reflection of the light from the sun. That's why this story has importance.

One evening Mother and Dad were sitting in lawn chairs enjoying the cool summer breeze. Dana sat in Mother's lap listening to the story about how God made the world.

Mother was right in the middle of her story when Dana spied the moon making its way up into the sky. Somehow it looked different. It looked more like a tipped saucer than a round moon. Dana grabbed Mother's arm. Then she pointed to the sky.

"Mummy, look!" she cried excitedly. "The moon's broke."

Something to Think About: Dana didn't know that during a certain time of each month the earth gets between the sun and the moon. When it does, it cuts off and hides part of the sun's light. The part that is hidden is not reflected by the moon.

But that doesn't mean that the moon is broken. It's one of God's rules that anything He made never changes. Everything works for us just as He planned it should. In the spring grass grows, trees get their leaves, and the birds come back to their summer homes. We can always depend on this being true. The sun shines every day, too, even though the clouds often get in the way so we can't see it. And, we know that daytime always follows night. This is another one of God's unchanging rules.

Still more important is the fact that God's love is always the same, too. Yesterday, today, forever, He is our unchanging loving Heavenly Father.

Bible Verse: "Every good and perfect gift is from God who never changes" (James 1:17).

Prayer: Dear Heavenly Father, we thank You for the wonderful world You have made for us. We thank You for the sun that shines every day. We thank You for grass and flowers and trees. We thank You that your love for us is always the same. Help us to show others we love You, too. In Jesus' Name. Amen.

First Steps

Have you ever watched a small baby who is learning to walk? If you have, you know how everyone holds his breath as the baby takes his first steps. Usually Mother stands near by. Sometimes she puts out her hand so the baby can get hold of one of her fingers.

Learning to walk isn't as easy as it seems. As long as the baby keeps looking at Mother, everything goes well. But when he looks at his feet, he usually falls.

But Mother is always ready to lift him up and get him started again. No one scolds. Everyone knows this is the way a baby learns to walk.

Then comes the happy time when baby takes his first steps, all by himself. "That's fine," everyone shouts.

After the first time, it is easier. There may be a few more spills. But they happen less and less often. Soon baby can walk and run all over.

Something to Think About: A baby's learning to walk is very much the same as learning to walk as a Christian. When we first accept Christ, we are told we are "babes" in Christ. We will make mistakes just as baby did. It isn't easy to change our habits overnight. There may be times when we get angry; when we are jealous; when we speak unkindly. Those are like falls. But we won't stop trying to be a good Christian just because of them. We get up and start all over again. Reading God's Word will help us in our walk. Prayer will help us, too. So will talking to our parents and to other people who know and love our Lord.

Bible Verse: "If we walk in the light as he is in the light, we have fellowship one with another and the blood of Jesus Christ cleanseth us from all sin" (I John 1:7).

Prayer: Dear Lord, help us to follow in Your footsteps. Then we know we will not fall along the way. We thank You that You have said we can come to You for forgiveness when we fail. Help us to start each day as a new walk with You. In Jesus' Name. Amen.

It Would

Someone has said Jason was the boy who gave Jesus the loaves and the fishes to feed the many people who had come together to hear Him preach.

The sun was sinking in the west and it made a rosy, pinkish glow across the whole sky. The people sat around in groups. They were no longer hungry because they had been fed.

Jason's mind flashed back to the time when he had joined the crowd. He was standing at the very edge looking up at Jesus when he felt an arm placed on his shoulder. The man led him through the crowd. And before he knew it had happened he was standing right next to Jesus. Jason learned the man's name was Andrew. He still didn't know just how it had happened, but he was asked if he would share his lunch with Jesus. Of course he would! Then the miracle happened.

With his own eyes he saw Jesus bless the food. Before long everyone had been fed. But there were twelve baskets left over. Jason looked at them now. Finally his curiosity got the best of him. He tugged at Andrew's sleeve.

"Sir, I've been wondering. Would it be that way with everything I gave him?"

Andrew looked at Jason. A broad smile cut across his suntanned face.

"Yes, my son," Andrew said. "It would. I know it would."

Something to Think About: No doubt Andrew had heard Jesus talk about people doing things for Him. Once He said that those who served Him would be rewarded sixty times, even a hundred times more.

Farmers know what this means. They plant a seed in the ground. Let's suppose it is corn. When it comes up the stalk produces a whole ear of corn. The one kernel has been increased many times. It's that way with the blessings we get when we serve Jesus, too.

Bible Verse: "Give and it shall be given to you, good measure, pressed down and running over" (Luke 6:38).

Prayer: Dear Heavenly Father, we thank You for the story of the boy who gave his lunch to Jesus. We thank You that we can do things for You, too. Bless us so we are blessed to running over. Then we can show others how much we love You. Forgive us our sins. Cleanse our hearts this day. In Jesus' Name. Amen.

Why Perry Was Glad

When Perry came home from his first day in school he was very excited. Last year he had been in kindergarten. Now he was in the first grade. And, best of all, Miss Browne, last year's kindergarten teacher, was going to teach the first grade.

"Mother!" Perry called as he ran through the house.

"I'm here, in the sewing room," Mother answered.

Perry hurried into the sewing room.

"Mother, do you know what?" he asked excitedly.

"No, what?" Mother answered.

"Miss Browne is my teacher this year, too. And, guess what? She knew who I was. Right away she said, 'Why hello, Perry, how are you?' "

Something to Think About: Why was Perry excited? Are you glad when people remember your name? Most people are. That's a lesson for you to remember. When you meet other children and especially older folks, be sure to get their name straight so you will know them the next time you see them. Older people love to have children call, "Hello, Mr. Peterson (or whatever the name may be)."

Something that is even more important is the fact that Jesus knows who you are. He knows your name. The Bible tells us this is true. And Jesus knows when we are sad. He knows when we are glad. He knows all about us.

Bible Verse: "The Lord is my shepherd, I shall not want . . ." (Psalm 23:1).

"He calleth his own sheep by name" (John 10:3).

Prayer: Dear Lord, we thank You for loving us as You do. We are glad You know us by name. Be with us this day wherever we go, whatever we say. We want to live to please and glorify You. In Jesus' Name. Amen.

The Littlest Candle

It was evening. Mother and Dad were reading the newspaper in the living room. Jeffrey and Dianne had just gone to their rooms to get ready for bed.

Outside the lightning flashed. The thunder rolled across the sky with a growling, grumbling noise. Then the rain came . . . buckets of it.

Jeffrey and Dianne liked to see the lightning flash through the edge of the window shades. They liked to hear the thunder roll.

"Boom!" Jeffrey growled mockingly as a sharp crash of thunder shook the house.

And strangely, just as he said, "Boom!" something happened. All the lights of the house went out.

"Electricity's gone," Dad called. "Stay where you are and we'll bring you some candles."

Jeffrey and Dianne heard Mother and Dad looking for candles. They heard several drawers open and close.

"Jim, I don't believe we have any," Mother said.

Then Jeffrey remembered something.

"There's a short one in my dresser drawer," he called. "I'll get it."

Dad hurried into Jeffrey's room. He scratched a match on the bottom of his shoe. Then he lit the candle and placed it in the candleholder Mother had given him. Right away a soft glow filled the room.

"Strange, isn't it," Mother mused. "A little candle, just about the littlest one I've ever seen, can give just as much light as a big one."

Something to Think About: This is something all children should remember. Did you ever sing the song, "This little light of mine; I'm going to let it shine. . . . Let it shine; Let it shine"? If you have, you know that you are the light that is going to shine for Jesus. And, just like the candle, a small person can give as much light as a tall one.

Bible Verse: "Young men and women, old men and *children* — Let them praise the name of the Lord" (Psalm 148:12, 13).

Prayer: Dear Lord Jesus, we know You are the Light of the World. We know that everyone who trusts You is a light, too. We thank You that it doesn't make any difference how young we are, we can still be a light for You. Help us to keep our lights burning brightly. In Your dear Name. Amen.

North Central Wool Marketing Corporation

Joel Calls His Sheep

One day a little shepherd boy named Joel found that the nine sheep his father had given him had strayed from their fold. Joel was sure someone had forgotten to close the gate.

Joel began to hunt for his sheep. To his surprise he found them with his neighbor's flock.

"Did you know my sheep are mixed up with yours?" he asked his neighbor shepherd.

"No, I didn't," the man answered. "That's really too bad. How will we find out which are yours? I am sure I can't tell them apart."

"Oh, don't worry," Joel said. "My sheep know me. If I call them, they will come to me."

The neighbor shepherd laughed. He didn't believe the sheep would answer Joel's call. But, he said Joel could try.

Joel stepped forward. He cupped his hands over his lips and began to call the names of his sheep. Sure enough, here and there a sheep began to push its way through the flock. In just a short time all nine of Joel's sheep had separated themselves from the others. When they saw Joel, they hurried to him. Joel started home and they followed him all the way to their fold.

Something to Think About: Jesus said He is your Shepherd and you are His sheep. He knows you by your name. Do you answer when He calls you? Do you follow where He leads you? Where does Jesus lead you?

Bible Verse: "And the sheep hear his voice and he calleth his own sheep by name and leadeth them out. . . . he goeth before them and the sheep follow for they know his voice" (John 10:3, 4).

Prayer: Dear Lord, You are our Shepherd. Because You are, You will always take good care of us. We are glad You know us by name. Help us to follow where You lead. Help us always to listen to Your call. In Jesus' Name. Amen.

The Man He Watched

When Henry Ward Beecher was a little boy, he used to sleep in a room across the hall from one in which the family's hired servant, a colored man, slept.

"I'm sure he never knew how often I watched him," Henry Ward Beecher once said. "But night after night, after I put out my light, I'd watch as he lay on his cot reading his Bible. Sometimes he would talk to himself about what he read. Sometimes he'd talk to God. Then, at other times, he'd chuckle happily about some verse he liked. In all my life, I've never seen anyone who enjoyed the Bible as he did. Right then and there I made up my mind that I would find out what there was in the Bible that my friend liked so well."

Henry Ward Beecher did find out why the Bible made his friend so happy. When he read it, it made him happy, too. Because it told about Jesus and His love for all men, Henry Ward Beecher became a Christian. Later he said,

"I believe more than anyone else our hired man helped me want to live for Christ."

Something to Think About: Did the hired man know that Henry Ward Beecher watched him? There will be many times when people will watch you, too. You may never know they are watching you. But what you do may make them decide whether or not they are going to follow Jesus. What does this teach you?

Bible Verse: "Let your light so shine before men that they may see your good works and glorify your Father which is in heaven" (Matthew 5:16).

Prayer: Dear Heavenly Father, help us to live day by day so we will show others that we are happy You are our Saviour. Help us never to do anything that would make someone else stumble and choose not to follow You. In Jesus' Name. Amen.

Bradley's Birthday Cake

It was Bradley's birthday. True to her promise, Mother began to bake him a birthday cake.

Bradley watched her eagerly.

Mother measured and sifted the flour. She creamed the butter and sugar and added the eggs. Into this mixture she stirred flour and milk.

Then she poured the batter into greased cake pans. Thirty-five minutes later the cake was done. She took the high, golden layers out of the oven. When they were cool, she covered them with fluffy pink frosting.

"Yummmy," Bradley exclaimed when he took his first bite of the cake. "How can eggs and flour, butter and milk be so good when they are mixed into a cake?"

Mother smiled wisely.

"I suppose it is because they are the right things to put into a cake. Then, too, they are mixed together in the right way."

Something to Think About: When the cake was finished, Bradley couldn't see the eggs, the flour, the milk, or the butter, could he? In a way a cake is like a person's life. If you want to make a good life you must put good things into it. You must read the right kind of books. You must think the right kind of thoughts. You must listen to the right kind of music. You must watch the right kind of television programs.

Mother would never put poison into her cake, would she? She wouldn't put dirt into the cake. Bad books, bad thoughts are poison.

Kindness, love, fair play, pure thoughts, and honesty are some of the things that help make a good life. Jesus says we should think about them and make them a part of our lives.

Bible Verse: "Whatsoever things are true, whatsoever things are honest, whatsoever things are just, whatsoever things are pure and lovely, think on these things" (Philippians 4:8).

Prayer: Dear Lord, You know how easy it is to let evil come into our lives. Help us to think about the things that are pure and lovely and kind. Help us to choose the right friends, the right books, the right television programs that will make us the kind of Christians you want us to be. In Jesus' Name. Amen.

Just a Little Thing

Mother had told Dale never to play with matches. But one day when mother was away, Dale set fire to some of the grass in the yard.

When the flames began to spread, Dale stamped on them with his feet. He hoped that would put out the fire. But when he stamped on the flames, his trouser legs caught fire. Soon all of his clothes were burning.

A neighbor ran to him with a blanket she had grabbed from her bed. She wrapped Dale in the blanket. When she wrapped him in the blanket, she smothered the flames. But Dale was already burned very badly. Another neighbor called the firemen to put out the fire.

Dale spent many, many months in the hospital. The doctors were able to heal his burns. Now Dale is well but he will always have a lame leg. The fire burned some of the muscles of his leg.

Something to Think About: Dale's trouble started with one small match. Just a little thing! But think of the harm it did. When someone tells you something doesn't matter because it's just a little thing, think about Dale. A small nail can puncture a big tire. A small hole sinks a big ship. Just so, a small sin can ruin a good life. A little lie can make people stop trusting you. Steal once and it is easy to steal again. Cheating just a little may not seem wrong, but it will make you grow up to be a cheating person.

Bible Verse: "Behold how great a matter a little fire makes" (James 3:5).

Prayer: Dear Jesus, we know that little things can cause a great deal of trouble. Help us always to think about this when we are tempted by little sins. Teach us to do what is right. In Your dear Name. Amen.

What a Leash Is For

Mother stood by the kitchen door. She was busy watching Linda who sat on the bottom step of the back porch. Linda held a long leash in her hand. A fat, black puppy played at the end of the leash. It romped on the grass while it chewed a toy bone.

"Why don't you let her go free?" Mother asked Linda.

"Oh, no!" Linda answered firmly. "I don't want her ever to know what it feels like to run away."

Tears came to Mother's eyes. She knew Linda was remembering another dog she had had. His name was Sambo. Both Mother and Dad had told Linda to keep Sambo on his leash. But Linda thought she knew better than they. Time after time she untied Sambo and let him run wherever he wanted in the yard.

One day he decided he wanted to go into the street, too. Linda called to him, but he pretended he didn't hear.

A speeding car hit the dog. Sambo was hurt very badly. After many days of suffering, he died. Linda cried and cried.

"If I ever have another puppy, I'm never going to let it know what it feels like to run away," she told her mother.

Now Mother could see Linda was keeping her promise. Mother walked down the steps and sat down beside her daughter.

"You have learned a very important lesson, Linda," she told her. "You have learned that too much freedom isn't good for a dog. He is little and doesn't understand the dangers of the street.

"I hope you have learned something else, too. I hope you have learned that when I say *No* to some things you want to do it is because I believe those things will hurt you. You see you aren't old enough to choose what is best. I suppose you could say you are on my leash. Understand?"

Linda smiled and nodded.

"I never thought about it like that before," she told her mother. "Now I know that's the way it has to be. I'll try to remember that I am on your leash when you tell me something is not good for me."

Something to Think About: How is a mother's care like a little dog's leash? Can you name times when you wanted to get loose from Mother's leash? Is Linda too strict with her little dog? Do you ever think Mother or Dad is too strict with you? Why do you think they are so strict?

Bible Verse: "Children, obey your parents in the Lord, for this is right" (Ephesians 6:1-3).

Prayer: Dear Lord Jesus, we thank You because You are the Son of God and our Saviour and Lord. We thank You because You love us. Help us to remember that too much freedom is not good for us. Help us to be glad to obey those who care for us. In Jesus' Name. Amen.

Jesus Our Guide

Baby Sue had just wakened from her nap. Mother began to dress her. She slipped a clean dress over her head. Then she put Baby Sue in her lap and pulled clean, pink stockings over her chubby feet.

"Now your shoes," Mother told her as she slipped them over the clean pink stockings.

But when she began to lace the shoes, Baby Sue shook her head and pushed Mother's hand away.

"Me do," she said in her little baby voice.

"All right, you do," Mother told her.

Baby Sue picked up one shoe lace. But instead of putting it in the right hole, she put it in the hole at the top of the shoe.

Mother smiled but didn't say anything.

Baby Sue picked up the other lace and pushed it through several holes on the same side of the shoe. Then she crossed the other lace and pushed the one she held through a hole on the other side.

It was a sorry sight. But still Mother didn't say anything.

Finally Baby Sue stopped. She tilted her head to one side and looked at the shoe. She wrinkled her forehead and scowled. Then she did something that surprised Mother.

She reached for Mother's hand. When she found it, she placed it on the shoe laces.

"You do," she told Mother.

Mother laughed as she began to untangle the laces. When she was through, she put her hand on top of Baby Sue's hand. She helped Baby Sue pick up the end of the one of the shoe laces. Then she guided the little hand so it pushed the lace through the right hole.

Criss-cross; criss-cross. Together Mother and Baby Sue laced the shoes as they should be laced. When they were through Baby Sue slid out of Mother's lap and ran across the room to play with her doll. Now she was happy. Mother had helped her lace her shoes.

Things were always right when she let Mother show her what to do.

Something to Think About: Why did Baby Sue need Mother's hand to guide her? Why did the shoes have to be unlaced before they could be laced correctly? Jesus said, "I will guide you with my eyes." How is Jesus like Baby Sue's mother? When we get things tangled up, when we make mistakes, to whom can we go to have them straightened out again?

Bible Verse: "I can do all things through Christ who helps me" (Philippians 4:13).

Prayer: Dear Lord, we thank You that You know all about us. We thank You that when we do things that are wrong we can come to You and ask You to forgive us. We know then that everything will be all right. Be our Guide this day. Help us to do what is right. In Jesus' Name. Amen.

A Poor Trade

Abraham Lincoln, the man who was President of the United States many years ago, had two sons, Robert and Tad. One day he gave Tad a pocketknife, the first Tad had ever owned.

The next day as Mr. Lincoln and a friend were walking along chatting together, they stopped to talk to Robert and Tad. Mr. Lincoln asked Tad to show his friend his pocketknife.

Tad scuffed the toe of his shoe into the dust along the sidewalk. He didn't look up at his father.

"Come, boy," Mr. Lincoln said. "Show the gentleman your pocketknife."

Feeling very ashamed, Tad told his father he didn't have it any longer. He had traded it with his brother for some candy.

Lincoln took time right there to show the boys what a poor deal Tad had made. The knife was worth much more than the candy.

By that time Robert began to feel ashamed, too. Suddenly he reached into his pocket and brought out the pocketknife. He handed it to his brother.

"Now, Tad, what about your part?" Mr. Lincoln said. "You got your knife back, now you must give back the candy."

Tad dug his toe into the dust along the sidewalk again.

"I can't," he told his father. "I ate it."

The man who tells this story went on to say that Tad promised he'd buy some candy to repay Robert.

This poor trade reminds us of a Bible lesson Jesus taught. He told His disciples that many people trade their souls for something that isn't worth nearly as much. They forget God. They may spend a lot of time at their business. They may waste time in foolish entertainment and sin. At the same time, they neglect going to church and worshiping God. That's really trading things of the world for friendship with God.

Something to Think About: Why do you think Tad made a poor bargain? What is the most important thing in the world? How can we lose it?

Bible Verse: "What shall a man gain if he gets the whole world but loses his own soul?" (Matthew 16:26).

Prayer: Dear Lord Jesus, we thank You that You are our Friend. We thank You for coming to this earth to save us from our sins. Help us to worship and love You always. Don't let us be careless and trade our souls for something that won't be of any value when we get to heaven. In Jesus' Name. Amen.

Follow the Leader

An Alaskan missionary is said to have owned a fine dog team. The dogs in his team were called "huskies." When harnessed to a sled, they pulled the missionary over the ice and snow. They helped him carry the story of Jesus to people in faraway villages.

As is always true in a team of huskies, one dog was trained to be the leader. One day the missionary decided he should train another dog to be a leader, too. Then if the first dog ever got hurt or became sick, he would have a dog who could take the leader's place. With this in mind, he took his best dog and placed him second in line in the dog team. He put his second dog at the head of the team.

From the very start he had trouble. The "lead" dog grew so jealous he dropped to the ground and would not move. When the missionary made him get up, he chewed the harness that fastened him to the first dog. That freed him so he was once again the lead dog.

81

Then his master tried another plan. He took him away from the team and tied him up by himself while the new leader was being trained.

Even that didn't work. The dog who had been the leader refused to eat. He moped and pouted until he became very ill. He would have died if the missionary hadn't given him back his place in leading the dog team.

Something to Think About: Have you ever heard children say, "I won't play unless I can be *it*"? That's really what this lead dog was saying, wasn't it? But, we can't blame the dog too much. He had been trained to be the leader. He wasn't able to understand why another dog was put in his place.

As Christians, we must learn to follow as well as to lead. We can't always be *it*. Jesus said it is better to take the least important place rather than ask for one that is first. This is the unselfish way of life.

Bible Verse: "When you are invited, go sit in the lowest place, then the one who invited you may come and say, 'Friend, go up higher' " (Luke 14:10).

Prayer: Dear Lord Jesus. Thank You for giving up Your place in heaven to come to earth to live with men. Thank You for giving Your life so that those who love You can live with You forever. Help us to be happy even when we can't have the best place, when we can't be *it*. Teach us how to be unselfish Christians for Your sake. Amen.

The Wonder Ball

Had you been a girl in Germany years ago, you would have learned to knit when you were very young. German mothers had a scheme by which they made their children want to learn to knit. When they wound the skeins of yarn into balls, they made what they called a "wonder ball." As they shaped the ball, winding the yarn round and round, they hid surprise gifts in the strands of wool — a penny here; a thimble there; a ring someplace else. The best surprise of all was placed in the very center of the ball.

Almost every little girl wanted to learn to knit. You see, when she knitted she just naturally used up the yarn on the ball. The more yarn she used, the more surprises she found.

When you stop to think about it, you will realize that God has a "wonder ball," too. *Time* is the wool that shapes His ball. And every day as we unwind that yarn we find surprises He wants us to enjoy.

Good health is a prize. So is sunshine; so is friendship; so are books and flowers. . . .

And just as the best treasure was placed at the very center of the ball, at the end of the yarn, God's best gift, heaven, is waiting for us when we've used up all of the yarn called TIME.

Something to Think About: Most people call God's gifts "blessings." You no doubt know the song, "Count your many blessings, name them one by one." When you pray, try thanking God for the blessings He gives you, naming them *one by one*.

Bible Verse: "Yes, the Lord shall give what is good" (Psalm 85:12).

Prayer: Dear Lord God; we thank You for all the blessings You have given us. We thank You for (*name them one by one*). In Jesus' Name. Amen.

Thank You, God

Sunday school teachers are wonderful people. They teach boys and girls about Jesus Christ.

This story is about a Sunday school teacher named Mr. Wordsworth. Because he loved the boys he taught, he was always trying to teach them some important lesson about God.

One warm summer day he invited them to his house for a picnic. The boys were delighted. Mr. Wordsworth had a big yard where they orten played games. Besides, he had one of the most beautiful flower gardens in the whole city.

The boys hurried to Mr. Wordsworth's home at the time he had suggested.

Mr. Wordsworth let them play by themselves for a while; then he called them to join him in the garden.

They walked past the rose bushes, past the gladiolas, past a bed of daisies. Then all of a sudden one of the boys let out a low, soft whistle. This was followed by other whistles. The boys could hardly believe their eyes. Here was a whole bed of flowers, each section a different color. That wasn't surprising. The thing that caught their attention was that each section spelled one of the boys' names. There was Jerry's name in purple flowers, Tom's in orange blooms, Jack's in yellow. No boy had been missed.

Mr. Wordsworth acted surprised, too.

"Well, what do you know?" he said. "Look what has happened to my flowers."

Jack, who usually spoke first, blurted, "Ah, come now, Mr. Wordsworth. You know you planted them."

"Oh, no," the teacher told him. "They just happened to grow that way."

But, the boys couldn't be fooled. They knew Mr. Wordsworth was just kidding. They knew seeds don't fall into the ground and make a pattern that way.

Something to Think About: The boys didn't realize it at first, but Mr. Wordsworth taught one of his best lessons in his garden that day. "When you get older," he said, "some people will tell you there is no God. They will say the sun, the moon, the earth,

84

and the stars just happened. Now you will know this is not true. As soon as you saw your flower names, you knew someone had to place the seeds to make the letters grow that way. So, when you see how the earth is formed; that day is always day and night always night; that spring follows winter; when you look at the mountains, the trees and the birds of the air you will know that Someone made them, too. That Someone is God."

Bible Verse: "In the beginning God created the heavens and the earth" (Genesis 1:1).

"The heavens show the glory of God and the earth proves He made it" (Psalm 19:1).

Prayer: Dear God, thank You for making such a wonderful world for us to live in. Thank You for the stars that shine at night. Thank You for the birds of the air, for the flowers that grow in such beautiful colors, for the trees that shade our land. Thank You, God, for everything. In Jesus' Name. Amen.

Give-Away Talk

Dad Browne brought a friend of his home for dinner one night. His name was Mr. MacDougal. He had just arrived in the United States from Scotland.

Mr. MacDougal and Dad had known each other in college and hadn't seen each other since. The two men were very happy to be together again.

Patty and Dean had often heard about Mr. MacDougal. Now they were glad he had come to visit their father.

Mother prepared Dad's favorite dinner and before long they were all sitting around the table listening to Mr. MacDougal tell about his land. Suddenly Patty asked.

"Mr. MacDougal, do all the people in Scotland talk the way you do?"

Mother nudged Patty's leg with her toe. Patty knew that meant she shouldn't ask questions like that.

But Mr. MacDougal didn't seem to care. He laughed merrily.

"You are right, my lass," he said, rolling his r's and pronouncing "lass" almost like "loss." "Everyone in Scotland talks like this. And do you know what?" His eyes sparkled mischievously as he asked the question. "If you came to Scotland, folks would know right off you were from New England."

"How come?" Patty wanted to know.

"Because you talk like a New Englander, that's why," Mr. MacDougal told her, mocking the New England way of speaking.

Something to Think About: When the maid heard Peter deny the Lord in the courtyard, she knew right away he was from the area around Lake Galilee.

Besides giving away a person's birthplace, speech also tells what a person is like. People who speak slowly usually act slowly, too. Those who run their words together are apt to be quick and excitable.

Our speech gives away our relationship to Christ, too. If we talk about others, if we use bad language, if we sass, we let people know that our speech isn't controlled by God.

Bible Verse: "Out of the abundance of the heart, the mouth speaketh." (What you love with your heart will be shown by how you talk.) (Matthew 12:34)

Prayer: Dear Lord, fill us with Thy love so that when we speak people will know we belong to You. In Jesus' Name. Amen.

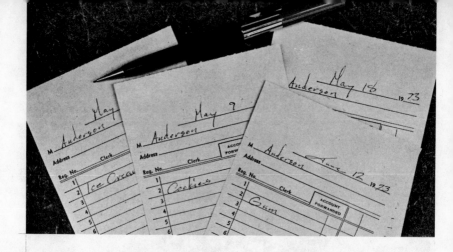

Scott's Charge Account

The Andersons live in a small town almost in the middle of the United States. There are five people in the Anderson family — Dad and Mother, Scott, Ann, and Terry.

Mr. Anderson owns a filling station in the town where they live. He often lets the farmers charge the gas they buy. That means he keeps a record of all they get. Then at the end of the month they come in and pay what they owe. A friend of Mr. Anderson, a Mr. Clark, owns a grocery store in the same little town. He lets folks charge their groceries, too. At the end of the month they are supposed to come in to pay him what they owe him.

As a rule, the Andersons charge their groceries at Mr. Clark's store. But, believe it or not, it was this charge account that caused a lot of worry one day.

One evening Dad called Scott, Ann, and Terry into the kitchen where he and Mother were going over the month's bills.

The children could see that something was troubling their parents. Dad bit his lip as he always did when he was puzzled. Mother looked worried.

"Is something wrong?" Terry asked.

Dad cleared his throat. He picked up a bunch of small bills that lay in front of him on the kitchen table. Very soberly he said,

"Yes, something *is* wrong. Mother and I have been going over our grocery bills and we find a lot of things have been charged that we didn't buy." He flipped his fingers through the bills. "Here's gum, 10¢; candy bars, 25¢; gum, 5¢; chocolate covered cookies, 35¢; ice cream bars, 30¢." He stopped and looked at the children. "Now who do you suppose has been charging these things on our bills?"

Terry shrugged his shoulders and looked at Ann and Scott. Ann shrugged her shoulders and looked at Terry and Scott. Scott didn't look at either of them. He looked down at his shoes. Nervously he began to trace around the linoleum pattern with his toe. Time seemed to stand still. But no one spoke.

Suddenly, Scott turned. In a wild lunge he threw himself into his mother's arms.

"I did it. I charged those things," he sobbed. "And I'm sorry."

"I'm glad you told us," Father told Scott. "But just saying you are sorry doesn't pay for the things you charged."

"But I haven't got any money," Scott whispered, his voice choked with tears.

"You have your allowance," Dad told him. "Now, if Mother will agree, this is my plan. I'll tell Mr. Clark to put these things on a separate bill for you. Then every week after you have given God what belongs to Him, you must give what is left to Mr. Clark. You must do this every week until the bill is paid. Understand?"

Scott nodded. He understood. To tell the truth, it was a lesson he never forgot. Terry and Ann never forgot it either.

Something to Think About: Why was it wrong for Scott to charge candy, gum, ice cream, and cookies? Do you think his father had a right to make him pay it back? Why was Mother worried? Scott asked his mother and father to forgive him. He asked God to forgive him, too. Our verse said he was blessed then. What does the word, "blessed," mean?

Bible Verse: "Blessed is he whose sin is forgiven" (Psalm 32:1).

Prayer: Dear God, we thank You that Your Word teaches us to be honest in all things. Help us to admit our mistakes when we make them. Help us never to be too proud to ask others to forgive us. Teach us to do Thy will. In Jesus' Name. Amen.

They Lost Their Way

Dad, Mother, and Danny Dickson were returning from a dinner to which they had been invited. They left the big city where their friends lived and headed home.

"Now, let me see," Dad Dickson said. "If I take the road that goes around the airport, I should be able to cut off several miles. We can hit the highway on the other side someplace, I am sure."

"Sounds like a good idea," Mother said. "But don't you think you should look at a map first?"

"No, I'm positive I can do it," Dad told her.

It was a beautiful evening. The sun had set but whenever Dad came to a curve in the road, the headlights made the red and orange leaves of the trees look like a huge bonfire. The Dickson family loved the country, especially in the fall. They chatted happily as they drove along the road Dad had taken. Up hills, down valleys, around curves, the car sped on its way.

After about an hour, Dad made a strange noise with his throat. "Hmmmmmmm," he said. "This is odd. We should have been on the main highway long ago. I can't imagine why we aren't there. Maybe you should look at the map, Mother."

Mother started to unfold the map. But she didn't get the first fold opened. Danny grabbed her shoulder just then and pointed ahead of the car.

"Look, Mom; look, Dad!" he cried excitedly. "Isn't this the place we started from?"

Danny was right. Somehow they had gone around in a circle and had come right back to the place from which they started.

"Well," Dad said, pulling the car to the side of the road. "Guess we'd better do some investigating." He reached for the map. "I was wrong," he said, after he had looked at the map. "The map shows the best way is to follow the main highway all the way."

90

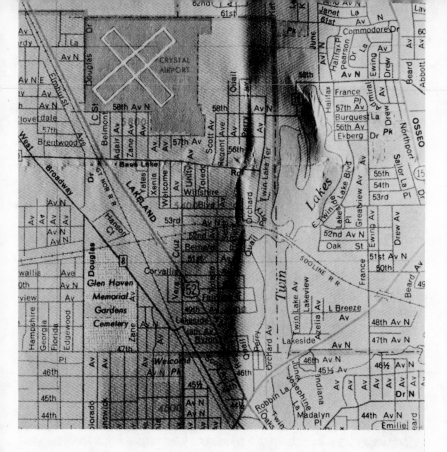

Something to Think About: Mr. Dickson did as so many people do. He thought he could take a shortcut home. He didn't even look to see where the map told him to go.

There is a song that says, "Heaven Is My Home." It is, too. It is our *eternal home*. Speaking about it, Jesus said, "There is no shortcut. I am the Way." He warned that some people would try to go around some other way. But that won't work. All of us have to follow His map. We must go the way He has planned for us to go.

Bible Verse: "I am the way, the truth and the life, no man cometh to the Father but by me" (John 14:6).

Prayer: Dear Jesus, thank You for the Bible, the Sunday school, for parents who teach us the way to the Father. Help us to trust You all along the way. Show us the danger of taking shortcuts that lead us in the wrong path. In Your Name. Amen.

Different Ice Cream Cones

It was a hot, muggy evening in July. Dad had been playing catch with Judy and Jerry. Now everyone was tired.

"Say, kids," Dad began. "How would you like to take a little drive? Maybe we could stop for some ice cream along the way."

Judy and Jerry thought this was a wonderful idea.

"Get Mother," Dad said, "then go and wash your hands while I drive the car out of the garage."

The cool air felt wonderful. Dad and Mother, Judy and Jerry drove along the river road south of their little town. On the way back they stopped for some ice cream cones.

"I want chocolate," Judy cried.

"I want strawberry," Jerry cried.

"And you, Mother?" Dad asked.

"Make mine vanilla," Mother answered.

When Dad came back with the cones Jerry asked, "What kind did you get, Dad?"

"My favorite, butter pecan," Dad told Jerry.

No one spoke for a time. Everyone was busy eating ice cream. Suddenly Judy broke the silence.

"Isn't it funny?" she said. "We all asked for different kinds of ice cream."

"Why not," Jerry asked. "We're different people, aren't we?"

Something to Think About: Jerry proved he was wise when he answered Judy as he did. We are different people. No two of us are exactly alike. Each of us has different likes and dislikes. We have different needs, too.

Did you notice how sure each member of the family was to name exactly the kind of ice cream he liked best?

This is a good lesson to remember when you go to God in prayer. You should learn to name the things you want God to help you overcome. You must ask forgiveness for *your own sins*. Name them one by one. And when you thank God, name the things for which you are thankful.

Some people pray, "God bless all our missionaries. God bless all our relatives. Forgive my sins."

It is better to say, "Bless Aunt Jane today." And if she is ill, pray, "Make Aunt Jane well." Name the missionaries you want the Lord to bless. If you know their special need, tell God about it.

Then, too, you are the one who really knows where you have failed God. You, too, know what are *your* special temptations. Ask God to help you overcome them.

Bible Verse: "In *everything* with prayer and thanksgiving let your requests be made known to God" (Philippians 4:6).

Prayer: Dear Heavenly Father, we forget that we should talk to You about our own needs. Forgive us. Help us to pray for our friends, our relatives, and missionaries according to their needs. Help us to thank You for *all* the things You have done for each one of us. In Jesus' Name. Amen.

When We Make a Mistake

Baby Sue came running to her mother. Her big blue eyes sparkled merrily. On her mouth was a great big smile.

"Well, Sue," Mother said as she stooped to pick her up. "What makes you so happy?"

Baby Sue chuckled and pointed to her sweater.

"Me do," she said proudly.

Mother looked where Sue was pointing. To her surprise she saw that Baby Sue had buttoned her sweater all by herself.

"Good girl," Mother said.

But, looking again, Mother saw that the buttons and button holes didn't come out even. There were two holes at the bottom of the sweater that didn't have any buttons.

"Look, Sue," she said. "You skipped a couple of buttons."

Baby Sue looked at her sweater. Her bottom lip trembled. She looked as though she were going to cry.

"Now, now," Mother comforted. "Don't feel so badly. We can fix it."

Mother helped Baby Sue unbutton the sweater to the place where the buttons had been missed.

"Now start again," she told her. "This time be careful not to skip a single button."

Baby Sue did as Mother said. Then, wriggling out of her arms, she ran to show Daddy what she had done.

Something to Think About: Why was Baby Sue so happy when she ran to her mother? What made her unhappy? Do you think mothers should tell their children when they make mistakes? Why? How did Baby Sue correct her mistake?

Going back to make things right is always the best way. Sometimes we say or do things that make other people unhappy. The only way to make things right is to go to them and ask forgiveness. We can never really be happy unless we know our sins have been forgiven.

Bible Verse: "Happy is the man whose sins are forgiven" (Romans 4:7).

Prayer: Dear Heavenly Father, help us to see our mistakes when we make them. Make us willing, too, to admit we made them. Help us always to ask the people we wrong to forgive us. In Jesus' Name. Amen.

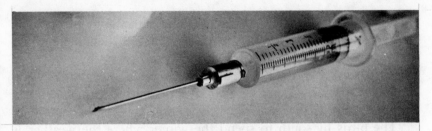

In Everything Give Thanks

Marlene had been very ill with whooping cough. When she first began to cough, Mother took her to the doctor. He knew right away what was wrong with her. He said he couldn't cure her cough, but he could make her better with some "shots."

Mother said he should give Marlene the shots.

The doctor did this.

Marlene didn't like the shots, though. That night when she prayed her evening prayer, she said,

"Dear Lord, I thank You for Mother and Daddy. I thank You for baby brother Joe. I thank You for being my Saviour.

"Bless all my friends . . . bless Jane and Susan . . . bless Mary and Judy . . . but don't bless Dr. Wilmott."

Something to Think About: Do you like Marlene's prayer? What is wrong with it? Why didn't she want God to bless Dr. Wilmott?

Marlene is like many people. When God sends something they don't like into their lives they become unhappy and forget to praise Him. Many times the thing God sends them helps make better people out of them, just as the shots helped Marlene.

Bible Verse: "In everything give thanks, for this is the will of Christ for you" (I Thessalonians 5:18).

Prayer: Dear Jesus, help us to be thankful for everything in life. Teach us to love all men. In Your Name. Amen.

Birds on Wing

Have you ever wondered where the birds go when winter comes? Perhaps you have watched them build their nests. You have seen them as they fly around your yard.

Then suddenly, they are gone. Where did they go?

People used to think the birds curled up someplace like a bear and slept all winter. Now they know this is not true.

The birds fly south to spend the winter where the weather is warm. We call their flight "migration."

Jeremiah told about migration in Bible times when he said, "Doth the hawk fly by Thy wisdom when she stretches her wings toward the south?"

In that verse we learn it is God who has taught the birds to fly south.

Some birds fly thousands of miles over land and sea. Others don't go quite so far. How do they know where to go? We know now that God gave them that instinct (the natural knowing).

One man wrote a poem about birds in flight. He said, "He (God) who guides the birds from zone to zone can guide our flight right, too."

Something to Think About: Do you believe God can guide us as He guides the birds? When we say God *can* guide us we are really saying He can guide us *if* we let Him. Each of us was born with a mind that says "Yes" or "No" to God. People who disobey God don't let Him guide them. But if we obey Him we can expect Him to help us to know which is the right way to go.

Bible Verse: "In all your ways acknowledge (obey) Him and He (God) will guide your way" (Proverbs 3:6).

Prayer: Our Father who art in heaven, we praise You because You are our God. Help us to obey You. Then guide our paths as You guide the birds of the air. Show us the right way to go. Amen.

The Very Best Gift

Do you know what a cartoon is?

You can find cartoons in almost any magazine. A cartoon is a picture drawn to tell a story.

An interesting cartoon you should know about was printed in one of the big magazines one Christmas.

Here is the story behind the picture.

It seems that a small boy didn't know what to give his mother for Christmas. Finally he had an idea.

He took a big cardboard box and cut two holes in the bottom. He climbed inside of the box and put his legs in the holes. Then peeking through a slit in the edge of the cover he walked to the front door. He reached one hand out and pressed the door bell.

Mother hurried to the door. When she opened it, her little boy called, "Merry Christmas, Mother."

Mother lifted the cover. Sure enough, inside of the box was her little boy.

"I didn't know what to give you for Christmas," he said. "So I decided to give you myself."

Something to Think About: Whose birthday do we celebrate at Christmas? Does He deserve a gift? Why don't you give Him the same kind of a gift the cartoon boy gave his mother? That would be the best gift of all.

Bible Verse: "They first gave themselves to the Lord" (II Corinthians 8:5).

"I want you to give your bodies to the Lord, for this is expected of you" (Romans 12:1).

Prayer: Take me just as I am, Lord. I give myself to You. I want to love and serve You with any talent You give me. Forgive my sins and cleanse my heart. In Jesus' Name. Amen.

Caught Napping

It was a beautiful day in May. Mother had gone shopping. Before she left she told Tom and Mary to make their beds. She told them to put the butter and milk in the refrigerator; to stack and wash the breakfast dishes.

Mary and Tom promised Mother they would have the house nice and clean when she came home.

They really meant it, too. But Mary began to read a new book she had brought home from the library. Tom went outside to play with the new puppy. He meant to stay outdoors just a little while. But he forgot all about the time. It was so much fun to romp and play with the puppy.

Time passed.

All of a sudden Mother drove into the driveway. When she reached the house, Mary was busy putting the butter and milk in the refrigerator.

"Oh, Mother," Mary said. "I didn't expect you home so soon. I got started reading my book and I forgot all about doing the things you told me to do."

"And you, Tom?" Mother asked. He had followed her into the kitchen.

Tom hung his head.

"I forgot, too. I was playing with the puppy."

Something to Think About: When Jesus returned to Heaven after He had risen from the dead, He promised that someday He would come back again. He warned all of us to be ready when He comes.

He said some people would do as Tom and Mary did. They would forget He was coming again. At least they wouldn't expect Him so soon. That would mean they wouldn't be ready when He came. They would be caught "napping," we say. That would mean, too, that they wouldn't be living as He would want them to live.

Bible Verse: "Blessed are the people who when the Lord comes again he will find watching" (Luke 12:37).

Prayer: Dear Jesus, help us to live every day so that we will be ready to meet You when You come to earth again. Keep our lives clean and pure. Help us to be busy for You. In Jesus' Name. Amen.

God's Love Lasts

Marilyn's older sister, Jane, was pulling the daisy petals, one by one, off their stalk.

Off came one petal. "He loves me," Marilyn heard her sister say.

Off came another. "He loves me not." This time Jane added *not*.

"What are you doing?" Marilyn asked.

Jane laughed. "Nothing really," she said. "It's just that some people believe you can tell if someone loves you with a daisy. If the last petal says, 'he loves me,' the answer is *yes*. If it says, 'he loves me not,' the answer is *no*."

Marilyn thought this was very interesting. The next day she decided she would try the daisy test of love.

"He loves me," she said as she pulled off a daisy petal. "He loves me not." She pulled another. One by one the petals fell to the ground. As she pulled the last petal away, she heard herself say, "He loves me not."

"Oh, my!" Marilyn cried. "I must tell Mother."

Marilyn ran to her mother.

"Mommy," she exclaimed, "God doesn't love me anymore."

"Why, Marilyn!" Mother said. "How can you say such a thing?"

"Well," she answered. "I tried Him on a daisy and the last petal said, 'He loves me not.' "

Something to Think About: Are you laughing at Marilyn? That's because you know God's love can never be tested by a daisy. His love lasts. It is for ever and ever. He never stops loving you.

Bible Verse: "Yes, I have loved you with an everlasting love" (Jeremiah 31:3).

Prayer: Thank You, God, for Your great love. Thank You for loving us before we learned to love You. Thank You for loving us so much that You sent Your Son to die for us. Help us always to love You, too. In Jesus' Name. Amen.

Telling Tracks

One morning Mother asked Dad to pick some tomatoes before he left for work. When he came back from the garden he said,
"The rabbits are getting your lettuce."

"Did you see one?" his son Bryant asked excitedly.

"No," Dad said. "I didn't. But I could tell the way the lettuce is nibbled that the rabbits have been in the garden. I saw their tracks, too."

Later that day, Mother called, "Bryant, come here."

Bryant ran to his mother.

"Haven't I told you to be sure to put the cover on the jam when you use it?" Mother asked.

"Hmmmhmmm," Bryant answered. "But how did you know I used the jam?"

Mother pointed to the refrigerator door. Close to the handle was a bright red smudge of raspberry jam.

"Some little boy left tracks behind him," she said.

In the afternoon of the same day, Bryant went with Mother to the store. When they came home they found a bouquet of lovely yellow roses on the back porch.

"Oh, oh," Mother said. "Mrs. Garret has been here."

"How do you know it was Mrs. Garret?" Bryant asked.

"Because she raises the most beautiful roses in the block. Besides, she is always doing something nice for her neighbors."

Something to Think About: How did Dad know a rabbit had been in the garden? How did Mother know that Bryant had taken some jam? Why did Mother think it was Mrs. Garret who had left the roses on the porch?

Some day when you think of it, go through the rooms of your house. Look around a bit. Can you tell by the things in the room who has been there?

It's that way in life all the time. We leave behind us things (tracks) that show not only who we are but what we are. The music on your piano and the records on your record player tell a good deal about you. The magazines and the books show whether yours is a family that loves the Lord or not. So do the pictures on your walls.

This shows how important it is that we leave the right tracks behind us. We help and hinder people by what we are.

Bible Verse: "Let your behavior be such that you will be a witness for God" (I Peter 2:12).

Prayer: Dear Lord, keep our lives clean and pure so those who come into our homes will know we love You. Help us to leave tracks that prove we belong to You. In Jesus' Name. Amen.

A Pretend Trip

One day Lowell, Lynn, and their friend Don built three automobiles in the back yard. The bodies of the cars were big wooden boxes. In each automobile they put an old chair. Some wheels on sticks were pushed into the ground to make steering wheels.

When the cars were ready, Lynn ran into the house.

"Mother, will you pack some lunch for us? We are going to take a trip."

Mother, who had seen the children make the cars, knew they would only be taking a pretend trip.

"Surely," she said. "I'll fix a lunch if you help me."

As they prepared the lunch — sandwiches, big red apples, cold lemonade in a thermos bottle — Mother asked about the trip.

"Where are you going?" she wanted to know.

"To California," Lynn told her.

"Do you know the way?"

"No, but Don does. He just came back from California. He's going to show us all the sights along the way."

Before long the children were settled in their make-believe cars. "Mmmmmmmmmm," they hummed as car motors do.

103

As they drove Don told them all about the towns through which they passed. Shortly before noon they got out of the cars. Mother saw them go into the cellar. She listened. They were pretending the cellar was a cave. Don was telling them all about the cave. He said that bats made their homes in the cave. Then he showed them the beautiful formations that hung from the ceilings.

In a little while they were on their way again. Other stops included the Grand Canyon, Boulder Dam, and the Redwood Forest. They ate their lunch in Los Angeles.

Later they drove into Mexico, then through Phoenix, Arizona, on to Colorado where they climbed Pike's Peak.

It was late afternoon when the children arrived back home. And that night when Mother tucked Lowell and Lynn in their beds they told her about the things they had seen.

Something to Think About: Have you ever taken a pretend trip? A pretend trip is fun as long as you know it is just make-believe.

Did you know that our lifetime is sometimes thought of as a trip? At the end of the trip we arrive in heaven. The trouble is, some people only take *pretend* trips to heaven. They act like they are going there. They go to church. They tell people they love God. But deep down in their hearts they know they are only pretending. God calls such people hypocrites because they pretend to be what they aren't.

Jesus tells us we should be sure we are taking a real trip to heaven. He says the Bible shows us the way. If we live as it tells us we can be sure that some day we will live with Him forever.

Bible Verse: "If we say we have fellowship with him and walk in darkness (without him) we lie and do not the truth" (I John 1:6)

Prayer: Dear God in heaven, we know that You know all about us. You know when we pretend to be something we are not. Help us always to be a true follower of Yours. Keep us from a make-believe Christian life. In Jesus' Name. Amen.

Straight Paths

A group of neighbor children had come together to play in the new-fallen snow.

"Let's see who can make a straight path across the field to the fence on the other side," red-haired Paul Matthews suggested.

"Let's!" the rest of the children cried as they plunged into the snow. But though they started out at a lively pace, they soon slowed down. The snow was deeper than they had thought.

But it wasn't long until everyone had reached the fence. Together the children turned to look at the tracks they had made.

They began to laugh. Almost all of them had zig-zagged across the field, making very crooked paths. That is, all except Tom Smyth, the new boy who had just moved into the neighborhood. Tom's path was as straight as an arrow flies.

"How come?" the children wanted to know.

"Well," Tom told them. "I picked out this fence post." He touched the fence post by his side. "Then I headed straight for it. I never once took my eyes away from it."

"I looked at my feet," Sarah Browne said.

"So did I," another youngster offered.

"That's why you went so crooked," Tom told them. "You have to have something to guide you if you are going to make a straight path."

Something to Think About: Why were most of the paths crooked? Why was Tom's path so straight?

A story in the Bible tells about the time Peter walked on the water when he was going to meet Jesus. As long as he kept his eyes on Jesus, everything went well. But, the moment he took his eyes off Jesus, he sank into the water.

This story is told so you will understand how important it is to keep your eyes on Jesus when you walk through life.

Bible Verse: "For this God is our God forever, and ever; he will be our guide even unto death" (Psalm 48:14).

Prayer: Dear Heavenly Father, we thank You that You are our God. We thank You for sending Jesus to be our WAY. We thank You that we can follow where He leads. Help us always to keep our eyes fastened on Him. In His blessed Name. Amen.

Meals Every Day

Tommy was in an ugly mood one morning when he came to breakfast. He sat down beside his sister, Ruth, plunked his elbows on the table and cupped his chin in his hands.

Mother put her finger over her lips, warning the rest of the family not to say anything, to pretend they didn't see how he was acting.

Mother knew what was wrong. Tommy had stayed up too late the night before. Mother and Dad had been gone and he hadn't put out his light when he was supposed to.

Now he was taking it out on his family.

Dad reached for the Bible as he always did each morning before they ate.

"Do we have to read the Bible every day?" Tommy blurted.

Dad looked at Tommy thoughtfully. Then, slowly, sadly he laid the Bible back on the shelf from which he had taken it.

"No, we don't *have* to read it everyday," he said. "That's one thing about God's laws. We can do anything we want to do. And if we don't want to read His Word, we don't have to."

Tommy looked surprised. But he didn't say anything. He was very quiet during the rest of the meal. He didn't eat much either.

When breakfast was over, Dad thanked God for the food, then excused himself saying he had to hurry to catch his bus.

Tommy may not have been hungry at breakfast time. But by noon he was starved. He hurried home from school wondering what Mother would have for lunch.

Tommy pushed open the kitchen door.

Funny, he thought. *The table isn't set.* He looked around. There was no food any place!

"Mom," he called.

"Yes, dear," Mother answered from the living room.

"Where's my lunch?" Tommy asked as he entered the room.

"There isn't any," Mother answered. "I didn't fix anything. I did a lot of thinking this morning and I decided we don't have to eat every noon. We don't have to eat every night, either. I

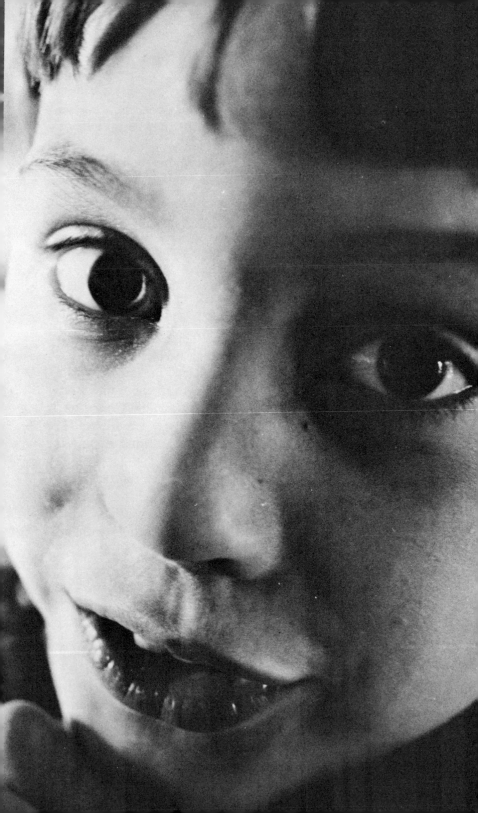

thought it might be a good idea if we didn't eat for several days."

Tommy looked at his shoes. He twirled his cap in his hands. He was beginning to feel very much ashamed. He knew what his mother was trying to tell him. And now he was sorry he had talked as he had at the breakfast table.

He ran to his mother and threw his arms around her.

"I'm sorry, Mother," he said. "I know we can't get along without food and we can't get along without the Bible either. We need it every day. Please forgive me for being so mean this morning."

Mother hugged her boy. Tears came into her eyes. But they were happy tears. She was glad her son had learned such an important lesson.

"Come," she said taking his hand. "What will it be, a tomato-bacon sandwich and a bowl of hot soup?"

Something to Think About: In the Old Testament we learn that God prepared a special food for His people as they traveled through the desert. It was a wafer-like food called "manna." God told His people they couldn't gather a whole month's supply at one time. They were to gather enough for each day, every day.

But, this was only food for their bodies. The New Testament tells us about food for our souls. There we learn that Jesus is bread from heaven.

If we don't eat food every day, our bodies will starve. If we don't read God's Word every day, our souls will starve.

Bible Verse: "Our fathers did eat manna in the desert. . . . this was not bread from heaven; but God gives you the true bread from heaven; for the bread of God is Jesus" (John 6:31-33).

Prayer: Dear Heavenly Father, we thank You because You chose godly men to write the Bible to tell us about Your love and care. Give us a real appetite for Your Word. Make us hungry for it every day. In Jesus' Name. Amen.

The Pumpkin Ghost

Aunt Esther was a writer. Mostly she wrote books for little children. Jane and Larry liked to read her books.

That's why they were so glad when they heard she was coming to visit them.

"I have a surprise for the children," Aunt Esther wrote Mother. "I have just finished a new book. It is a Hallowe'en book. But I won't tell anymore about it. I want Jane and Larry to read it themselves."

Sure enough, when Aunt Esther arrived she brought her new book with her.

·Right away Jane and Larry wanted to read it. As soon as they opened the pages, they began to laugh. "Oh, what funny pictures," Jane said.

"This is the best book yet," Larry told his aunt.

The story was about a family of ghosts who lived in the attic of an old house. They wore long white robes that looked like bed sheets.

This ghost family had a secret. They could change themselves into anything they wanted to be. Each ghost, Mother and Father, older brother down to the baby ghost, wore white pointed caps on their heads. Attached to the end of each cap was a string. When the ghosts pulled the cap string, they could change themselves into whatever they wanted to be.

110

The story was called "The Pumpkin Ghost" because on Hallowe'en the baby ghost changed into a pumpkin. The book told what happened to him when he did this.

The part of the story that interested Larry and Jane the most was the part that told about the string at the end of the white pointed caps.

"I wish we had a string to pull to change us into what we want to be," Larry said.

"And what would you want to be?" Aunt Esther asked.

"Oh, lots of things . . . a bear . . . a tiger . . . an eagle flying high in the sky," Larry answered. "And when I grow up, I could make myself into a doctor or a king . . . or even the President of the United States."

Something to Think About: We know Larry's wish for a magic string could never come true. But he said something we ought to think about.

What did he say he would like to be when he grew up?

Now Larry may not know it but he can become whatever he wants to be when he grows up. To do this he must begin now to plan to be that kind of person.

You can be anything you want to be, too. Right now you are making choices that decide what kind of person you will be when you are grown.

You may not know exactly what kind of job you will have. But you can decide right now to be honest, truthful, cheerful, helpful and unselfish. Then, if you practice being honest, truthful and unselfish every day, before long you will find out you are that kind of person.

If you are interested in certain work you can begin learning about that work.

Bible Verse: "I can do all things through Christ who gives me strength" (Philippians 4:13).

Prayer: Dear Jesus, help us to choose what is right for our lives. Help us to be honest, truthful, kind and unselfish. Lead us to the jobs You want us to do. In Your Dear Name. Amen.

A Secret to Tell

"I've got a secret I won't tell!"

Have you ever said those words?

Do you know what a secret is?

The dictionary says a secret is something that isn't known by others or something that is known by only a few people.

One day Jesus was moving through a crowd of people. A woman who had been sick for many years touched the hem of His coat. Right away she was healed.

Just think how happy she must have been. But the strange thing about her healing was that she decided to keep it a secret.

She didn't get to, though. Jesus knew someone had touched His coat. Turning, he asked,

"Who touched Me?"

The woman answered, "I did."

Something to Think About: What is a secret? If you had been this woman, would you have kept Jesus' healing a secret?

When we tell others what Jesus has done for us we are "witnessing" for Him. Witnessing about Jesus is always wise.

When the woman told Jesus He had healed her, the people in the crowd heard her, too. This was a good thing because they learned Jesus really could heal diseases.

We should never be afraid to tell others that Jesus has healed us of our sins. We should never be ashamed because we are Christians. There have been many times when children told about their love for Christ and others learned to love Him, too.

Bible Verse: "For I am not ashamed of the Gospel of Christ, for it is the power of God to save everyone who believes" (Romans 1:16).

"Whosoever will confess (tell others about) me before men, him will I confess before my Father in heaven" (Matthew 10:32).

Prayer: Dear Jesus, make us good witnesses for You. Help us always to be ready to tell others that we love You. Thank You for hearing and answering our prayers. In Thy precious Name. Amen.

Vaccinations

Weeding the garden, Mother could hear the children as they played in the sand box. Mary, from across the street, and Joe and Randy, from the house next door, had joined her Jennifer and Todd.

The children built roads and laid out sand-box cities in their play.

Suddenly Mary piped, "What's that on your arm, Joey?"

"That's my vaccination," Joe answered.

"Oh," Mary said. "Mine is on my leg. It shows when I wear my bathing suit."

"I wonder," Todd mused. "Why do we have to have vaccinations anyway?"

"It's so we won't get sick," Randy said.

"But I get sick," Jennifer offered. "I get colds and I've got a vaccination."

Mother decided it was time she stepped in. She left the garden and went over to where the children were playing. She sat down on the edge of the sandbox.

"Hi," she said. "I think I can tell you about vaccinations. The vaccinations you children are talking about are smallpox vaccinations. They don't keep you from getting colds but they do keep you from getting smallpox. Before vaccinations were discovered, many children died from this disease. Now smallpox is hardly ever heard of in this country. That's because so many children have been vaccinated against it. The medicine the doctor rubs into your skin at the vaccination spot keeps you from getting the disease."

Mother stopped. She let the children think about what she said. Then she went on.

"Wouldn't it be wonderful if we could be vaccinated against sin, too?"

"We can," Todd said.

"We can?" Mother asked. "How?"

"By letting Jesus live in our hearts."

Something to Think About: Have you been vaccinated against smallpox? What does the vaccination do for you?

Now, another question — have you been vaccinated against sin? Can this be done? What plan did Todd suggest?

Bible Verse: "Thanks be to God who gives us victory over sin" (I Corinthians 15:57).

Prayer: Dear Lord, we are thankful there is protection from smallpox. But, more important, we thank You because You protect us from sin. Bless our lives and help us to live for You. In Jesus' Name. Amen.

Everyday Bread

Susan and Trudy liked to watch Mother when she worked in the kitchen. They liked to watch her when she mixed cookies and cake. They liked the yummy smell that filled the kitchen when Mother baked bread.

One day when Susan and Trudy came home from school they found Mother busy decorating fancy sandwiches. They knew that meant she was getting ready for a party.

"Want one?" Mother asked.

Each girl helped herself to a sandwich.

Just then Dad came through the door.

"Want one?" Mother asked.

"No, M'am," Dad answered, a happy lilt in his voice. "When I eat sandwiches, I want them to be real he-man sized. I like bread that is bread."

Mother laughed.

"I can see your point," she said. "And, I see, too, why Jesus is called the Bread of Life. Certainly He is to be enjoyed at special occasions. But, He's good everyday bread . . . bread to be enjoyed all the time."

Something to Think About: Have you ever been in a home where bread was never served? No doubt you haven't, for bread is eaten by most people of the world. Small children, children in grade school, high school young people, and older folks all eat bread.

Wouldn't it be wonderful if everyone gave as much attention to Jesus who is the *Bread of Life* as they do to the bread they eat? Then people's spiritual bodies would be well fed, too.

Bible Verse: "I am the living bread which came down from heaven; if any man eat this bread he shall live with me forever" (John 6:51).

Prayer: Dear Heavenly Father, we thank You for all the food You have given us. We thank You for milk to drink, for vegetables, fruit and bread that help build strong bodies. Thank You, too, for Jesus who is the *Bread of Life*. In His Name. Amen.

A Father Has Time

Steve and his friend Craig were shopping for school supplies. When Steve came to pay the clerk for the things he had bought, he found he didn't have enough money.

"May I leave these things here for awhile?" he asked the clerk. "I know where I can get some money."

"Surely," the clerk told him.

"Come, Craig," Steve called as he started to leave the store.

The two boys hurried down the street. They passed the shoe store. They passed the post office. They walked until they came to the court house.

"Where are we going?" Craig asked.

"Wait and see," Steve answered taking the court house steps two at a time.

Steve led the way . . . through the big glass doors, down the marble hall. He stopped in front of a door at the very end of the hall. In big letters on the glass were the words, JUDGE OF PRO- BATE COURT.

Steve started to open the door. But Craig held back. When he spoke his voice was just a whisper.

"That's your dad's office, isn't it?"

"Sure," Steve answered. "So?"

"Are you allowed to go in to see him anytime?" Craig asked.

"Why not, he's my dad, isn't he?" Steve answered.

Something to Think About: This story reminds us of our Heavenly Father. He is a Judge, too. But, because we are His children, we can go to Him anytime.

It doesn't make any difference whether it is night or day, noon or night, you can talk to God when you want to. He is always ready to hear.

Bible Verse: "Let us therefore come boldly (without fear) to God and he will be kind and gracious to us" (Hebrews 4:16)

Prayer: Dear Lord God, Maker of heaven and earth, we thank You because You are our Father. We thank You because we can stop to talk to You anytime in the day or night. We can pray to You whenever we need Your help. In Jesus' Name. Amen.

Roots Before Flowers

Mark studied the green plant Mother had placed in a glass of water.

"What's the plant doing in the water?" Mark asked.

"Getting roots," she answered.

Mark looked puzzled.

"Are roots like flowers?" he wanted to know.

"No, dear, flowers grow above the ground; roots grow under the ground." She pointed to the tiny string-like shoots that were forming at the bottom of the plant. "They are roots," she said. "When there are enough of them, I will put the plant in some soil so it can grow leaves and flowers."

"Do all plants have to have roots before they can grow?"

"I believe so," Mother answered. "At least before they grow very much. Do you remember the rose bushes we planted last spring?"

"Sure, they were more roots than rose bushes, though," Mark told her.

"That's why they have done so well. It's the roots that collect food and water for the plants. If a plant didn't have any roots, it would soon wither and die."

Something to Think About: Boys and girls need roots, too, if they are to grow as they should. Good habits are good roots. Happiness is a good root. So is the right kind of education. But the most important roots are the ones that grow in Sunday school and church.

If you are trained to understand what is right and wrong, if you learn to love Jesus when you are young, when you are older you will grow into the kind of man or woman God wants you to be.

Bible Verse: "That Christ might live in your heart by faith, and that, being rooted and grounded in love, you will live a good life for Him" (Ephesians 3:17-19).

Prayer: Dear Lord, we want to be rooted and grounded in Thy love so we will always want to serve You. Bless us this day. Keep us from evil and harm. In Jesus' Name. Amen.

Whosoever Means You

To Laurine the best time of the day was story time. She especially liked when Daddy read to her. She liked the safe feel of his big lap. And, when she laid her head against his chest, she liked to hear the strong, sure beat of his heart.

Besides, Daddy had the best voice for reading stories. He made sounds exactly like the wind blowing in the trees. He could growl like a bear and chug like a railroad train. When he talked the part of the people, he made his voice just like theirs. And he could make his voice sound happy or sad, angry, faraway or close at hand.

Sometimes, though, Daddy played a trick on Laurine when he read to her. He'd be reading along about some little girl. Then suddenly, instead of saying the girl's name, he would put Laurine's name in the story. If there was a dog in the story, he would call it "Scratch," which was the name of Laurine's dog. If there was a father in the story, he might even call the father Mr. James, which was Daddy's own name.

This is how a story would sound —

"Very very early Sister heard noises in the kitchen. It sounded as though people were eating breakfast. So early?

"Sister jumped out of bed to see who was there. She ran down the steps, through the hall and into the kitchen.

"There sat Daddy and Jimmy. They were all dressed, ready to go fishing.

"So they were sneaking away without her. All at once Laurine *was very angry. . . ."*

The instant Daddy said her name, Laurine knew he was playing his trick again.

"Daddy!" she scolded. "You know that story isn't about me."

"Oh, so it isn't," Daddy would say. Then he'd begin reading again. But before long some one else's name would creep into the story.

"Daddy!" Laurine would scold again.

"Oh, dear," Daddy would say. "It's strange how our family manages to get into my stories."

118

Something to Think About: Have you ever tried putting your name in a story that was being read to you? Try it. It is great fun.

Now you know putting your name in a story doesn't really make you a part of the story.

But there is a story where your name does fit, though. That story is the Bible.

Think about the verse in which Jesus said, "I am come that you might have life." If Laurine put her name where the *you* is, it would read,

"I am come that Laurine might have life."

The reason this works so well with Bible stories is because the Bible was written for all people.

"*All* have sinned and come short of the glory of God," means all people have sinned and failed to please God.

"*Whosoever* will confess me before men, him will I confess before my father in heaven" means if *you* (put your name where *whosoever* is) will confess Jesus He will also confess you.

Try putting your name in some of your favorite Bible verses and you will see how well it works.

Bible Verse: "For God so loved the world that he gave his only begotten son that .... (*say your name*) believeth in Him should not perish but have everlasting life (John 3:16).

Prayer: Dear Heavenly Father, thank You for including each of us in Your plan of salvation. May we always seek Thy will for *our* lives. Keep us in Thy love. In Jesus' Name. Amen.

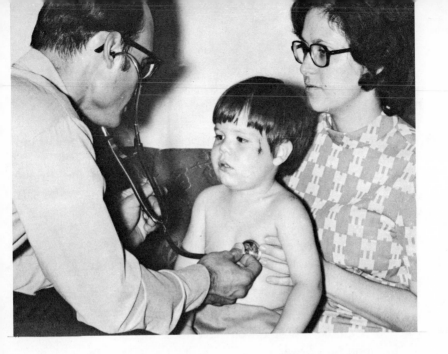

Doctor or God?

Joe Brinks liked to go to Sunday school. He liked the Bible stories he learned in Sunday school.

Joe always listened carefully when his teacher told about the things Jesus did for other people. He liked to hear how Jesus healed different kinds of diseases. There was one thing that bothered him, though. His teacher said God still heals people's diseases.

Joe was sure she was wrong about this. After all, he ought to know. His daddy was a doctor and Joe knew people came to him to be healed.

He wondered if his teacher knew this was so. He decided to tell her. One Sunday when she had finished telling a story about Jesus healing a blind man, Joe raised his hand. The teacher asked him what he wanted.

"God doesn't heal people now," he said. "My daddy does."

The teacher thought for awhile. Then she said,

"Joe, will you do something for me? When you go home ask your daddy if it is he or God who does the healing?"

Joe said he would do this.

As soon as he got home he told his father what the teacher had said.

"Don't you heal people?" Joe wanted to know.

"Yes, I do, Joe," his father answered. "But not alone. God helps me." Joe's doctor dad motioned him to come near.

"Come here, Joe, I'll show you what I mean." Dr. Brinks pulled back Joe's shirt sleeve. He pointed to the long white scar on Joe's right arm.

"Do you remember how you got that scar?"

"Sure," Joe answered, "I tumbled off my bike."

"Do you remember how your arm looked before I stitched and bandaged it?"

Joe nodded.

"Now suppose the cut had stayed exactly as it was when I stitched it closed. Would you have liked that?"

Joe shook his head.

"Did I do anything to the sore after it had been bandaged?"

"You just changed the bandages."

"Yet it healed. Who do you think made it heal?"

Joe was beginning to understand.

"It must have been God," he said.

"That's the way it is all the time," Joe's father told him. "I do the best I can. I take out little children's tonsils, but God heals the sore spot. I set broken bones, but I can't make them grow together again. God does that."

Something to Think About: God has given doctors a wonderful understanding of the human body. When we go to them, they tell us what is wrong. They may set a broken leg or arm. But it is God who finishes the healing.

Bible Verse: "Who forgives all your iniquities (sins); who heals all your diseases" (Psalm 103:3).

Prayer: Dear Lord, thank You for the doctors who help the sick. Thank You for the nurses who take care of the sick. Thank You, too, for being the great Physician (doctor). Thank You for healing our sins as well as our diseases. In Jesus' Name. Amen.

Ice Cream for George

"Larry Arden Anderson!" Mother's voice had that "what-are-you-doing-now?" sound.

And what was Larry doing?

Just a tiny boy, not far past the walking stage, Larry had pushed a chair over to the kitchen cupboards. He had climbed the chair. And somehow he had managed to open one of the cupboard doors.

On the counter in front of him was a big bowl.

Mother looked into the bowl. *Oh, my!* she thought. *What is that?* She could see some sugar in the bowl . . . and some flour . . . and rice krispies. But the smell? At first she couldn't tell what it was. And that oily substance? Ah, she had it. *Cod liver oil!* Strange, but true, Larry liked cod liver oil. *But why had he put it into this bowl?* Mother wondered.

"What do you think you are making, son?" she asked.

"Ice keem for George," he answered.

Mother laughed and laughed. George was Larry's favorite uncle. He had written that he was coming to visit. He would arrive at noon. And Larry had mixed some ice cream for him! At least he thought it was ice cream.

Mother scolded, but she didn't spank her little boy. She knew he loved George and in his own childlike way had decided to make something special to give him.

Something to Think About: We can laugh at this true story. But it does have a lesson for us. It shows us how a little boy wanted to do something for the man he loved so well.

Life is a matter of doing for others. The more we forget ourselves and think about what we can do for someone else, the happier we will be.

Jesus said if we do things for others, especially those who need our help, we are really doing it for Him.

Bible Verse: "In that you do things for the least of these, my brethren, you really do it for me" (Matthew 25:40).

Prayer: Dear Lord Jesus, help us to love others as You loved them. Help us to do good to all men. In Your Name. Amen.

The Very Best Friend

It was the first day of school.

Miss Browne, the teacher, asked the children to tell her what they had done during the summer months.

Mary Smyth said she had visited her grandmother on the West coast.

Jerry Barnes said he had visited an uncle in Chicago. His uncle had taken him to the beach. He had taken him to Brookfield Zoo and to a big museum near the lake.

Karl Duncan said he had spent the summer with relatives on a farm in central Iowa.

One after another the children told the teacher what they had done during the summer.

Then it was Kim Lu's turn. Kim Lu was a new little girl in the class. Her father was a dentist. Kim Lu was Japanese and all of her relatives lived in Japan.

What could she say? she wondered. She hadn't visited any relatives. She didn't have any relatives in America to visit. But she would have to say something. Suddenly it came to her what she could say.

"We didn't go any special place," she said. "That's because we moved here this summer. Besides, I don't have any aunts and uncles in this country."

She watched the other children. Someone snickered. This made Kim Lu very uncomfortable. Then she remembered. Friends were like relatives, weren't they?

"But we've got friends," she said. "We didn't visit them, they came to visit us."

Something to Think About: Kim Lu may not have realized it but she had something that is prized very highly. "Friends," someone has said, "are the fairest furniture of life." They are, if they are good friends.

What makes a good friend? Do you have friends? What must you do to have friends? Who is the best Friend of all?

Bible Verse: "You are my friends if you keep my commandments" (John 15:14).

Prayer: Dear God in heaven, thank You for Mother and Father. Thank You for all the members of our family. Thank You, too, for our friends. Thank You for Jesus who is the best Friend of all. Help us to be His friend by keeping His commandments. In His Name. Amen.

God Will Know

Mother was cross. Brad and Danny knew it the moment she called. Her voice sounded cross. Besides, she didn't say, "Brad and Danny, come here." She said;

"Bradley Ames! Daniel Philip! Come here this instant!"

Something must be wrong.

Brad and Danny hurried to the house.

"Where did you learn to use that kind of language?" she asked sternly.

"What kind of language?" Brad asked. Daniel looked puzzled.

"I heard you . . . when I was upstairs cleaning. The window was open."

Brad and Danny looked at each other. Right away they knew what she was talking about. Sometimes when they didn't think anyone was listening, they talked to each other in the rough, gruff way some of the boys at school talked.

"We didn't know you were listening!" Danny told his mother.

"And does that make a difference?" Mother asked. Her voice was softer now. "I'm just your mother. There is Someone much more important that hears every word you say. Do you know who that Someone is?"

The boys nodded. They knew Mother was talking about God.

Something to Think About: Someone has said, "We are what we are when we think no one is listening." This is true. Our real person shows up then.

Brad and Danny would never have talked as they did in front of their family. Yet when they were alone, they let the wrong words slip from their lips. They showed what they were really like when they were by themselves.

It's very important that we live good lives *all the time*. You see, God knows and hears wherever we are.

Bible Verse: "The eyes of the Lord are in every place, watching what is good and bad" (Proverbs 15:3).

Prayer: Dear Lord, help us to understand that You know and see everything we do. Keep us from evil always. In Jesus' Name. Amen.

Don't Mock God

Mother listened.

She couldn't believe her ears. Baby Sue sat on the living room rug playing with her doll. But it wasn't what she was doing but what she said that startled Mother.

Baby Sue was saying words that Mother had told her children they must never say. But, and here was the surprising thing, as soon as Baby Sue said a naughty word, she added, "Dear Jesus, forgive me."

Then she said another naughty word, and added,

"Dear Jesus, forgive me."

Why? Mother wondered.

Suddenly Mother remembered. Baby Sue must have heard her scold Brad and Danny for saying a naughty word. Mother had told them they must ask Jesus to forgive them for talking as they did.

And now, Baby Sue was asking Jesus to forgive her.

The bad thing about it was that she kept right on saying the naughty word. And each time she said it, she asked Jesus to forgive her. Mother decided she'd better have a talk with Baby Sue right then and there.

Something to Think About: We can understand why Baby Sue did what she did. She wouldn't know her brothers had promised God they would quit saying naughty words. She didn't understand that we can't ask Jesus to forgive us for something, then keep right on doing that thing.

That mocks God.

Suppose you broke your neighbor's window. You were truly sorry. You told your neighbor so and asked him to forgive you. Now what would your neighbor think if you kept right on breaking his window? Would that prove you were really sorry?

Bible Verse: "Blessed are they that hear my word and keep it" (Luke 11:28).

Prayer: Dear Father, forgive us our sins. Keep us from repeating what we know is wrong. Lead us this day. In Jesus' Name. Amen.

What It Is Like to Die

Greg stretched his arms lazily. Then he yawned. It was the big, wide yawn of a young boy awakening from a deep sleep.

Suddenly Greg sat up. Where was he? He expected to wake up in his own bedroom. That was where he had gone to sleep. Now he was in another bed.

All at once he knew. He was at Grandmother's. But how could that be?

Greg dressed quickly and ran downstairs to greet his grandmother.

"Good morning, Grandmother," he called as he entered the room. "How did I get here?"

Grandmother chuckled.

"Your folks brought you. They were called out of town because your Uncle Mac is a very sick man. Your father wrapped a blanket around you while you slept. He put you in the car and brought you here. You didn't once open your eyes.

"You'll be staying here until your folks get back. Okay?"

Greg smiled broadly. Okay was right. He liked being at Grandmother's house.

Something to Think About: Have you ever wondered what death is like? Then this story should help you.

If we love Jesus, we need never fear death. What will happen is that we will go to sleep here on earth in death. Then when we awaken, we will be with Jesus. We won't know how we got there . . . just as Greg didn't know how it happened that he was at his grandmother's. But we won't care a great deal. We'll be so glad to know we have arrived.

Bible Verse: "Yes, though I walk through the valley of the shadow of death, I will have no fear, for thou art with me . . ." (Psalm 23:4).

Prayer: Dear Jesus,
> Through this day be Thou with me
> Bless the friends I love so well;
> Take me when I die to heaven
> Happy there with You to dwell. Amen.

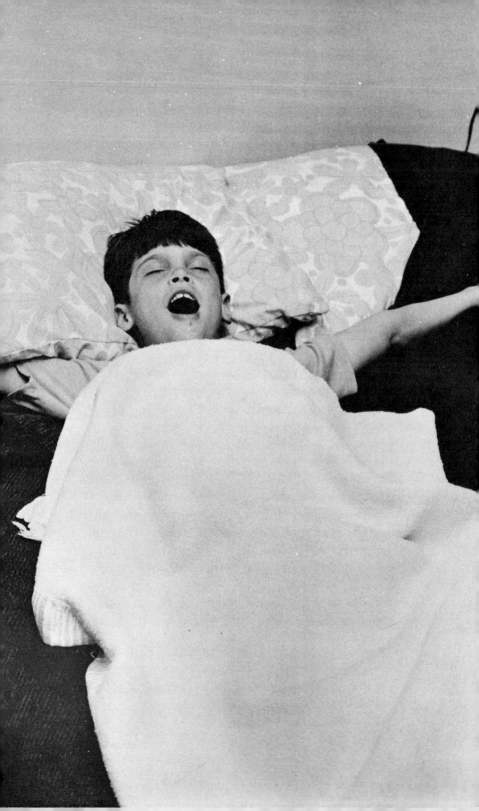

Ask Someone Who Sees

Beth lived close to a school for blind people. The school had been built to help the blind get used to not being able to see. Here people learned to read using the raised dot-letter books. They learned to type, to cook, to run office machines.

Quite often the school trained people who still had their sight but who knew they were going to lose it. The near-blind people had to learn to walk on a sidewalk. They had to learn to cross a street; how to get on and off a bus.

Beth liked to watch these people practice doing these things. Because the people could still see a little bit, the teacher put blindfolds over their eyes so they would know what it was like to be blind. Someone who knew the way always walked with the folks who had been blindfolded. They could help them if they needed help.

One day when Beth visited her cousin in the country, she told her about the school for the blind.

"I wonder what it would be like not to see," her cousin Anne said.

"I wonder, too," Beth said. "Say, we could find out. We could blindfold our eyes like they do at the school."

"Let's," Anne answered.

Before long two blindfolded children headed down the road toward the mailbox. Holding hands, they started out very slowly, feeling their way with careful feet. Then getting more courage, they began walking faster.

It took only a short time before both of the girls headed for the ditch.

"I guess only one of us should be blindfolded," Beth said. "Then one could see and show the other one the way."

Something to Think About: This story is much like one Jesus told His disciples. Often He likened physical blindness to the kind of blindness people have when they don't see or understand God's love and teaching.

In the story Jesus told, there were two men, both of them blind. They, too, fell in a ditch. Jesus said, "They are blind leaders of the.blind. And if the blind lead the blind, both fall into the ditch."

This is especially important for you to remember. Always go to the person who sees and understands God's teaching for the help you need in your own life. Someone else will lead you astray and make you lose your way.

This does not mean that all physically blind people are blind to God. Some of them see and understand Him better than those who can see with their eyes.

Bible Verse: "Evil men don't understand God's way but those who seek the Lord understand all things" (Proverbs 28:5).

Prayer: Dear Lord, we know there are many things we will need to know about You. Help us to understand that only those who know You can help us. Teach us Thy way. In Jesus' dear Name. Amen.

Get a Specialist

Phil and Brent were racing down the driveway on their roller skates. Suddenly Phil stumbled.

When he started to get up he found he couldn't. His arm hurt him terribly. Looking at it, he knew why.

By this time Brent realized Phil was not following him. He turned and skated back to his friend.

"What happened?" he asked.

"I think I broke my arm," Phil answered, biting his lip because of the hurt. "Please call my mother, will you?"

When Mother saw what had happened, she telephoned the doctor. He told her to bring Phil to his office right away.

On the way to the doctor's office, Phil asked,

"Can't you fix it, Mother?"

Mother reached over and touched Phil's knee. She smiled at him fondly.

"No, honey," she told him. "Neither you nor I could do much with that arm. That's a specialist's job."

Something to Think About: Why couldn't Phil set his own arm? Why couldn't Mother set it?

You know a specialist is someone trained to do a special kind of work. A doctor is a specialist in healing people's bodies.

A broken arm or leg is bothersome. But, according to Jesus, there is something much worse. That is a broken, sinful spirit.

Remember this when you find yourself doing things that you shouldn't do. You can't make things right when you sin. Mother can't fix them. You must go to a specialist. Who is He?

Bible Verse: "Thou shalt call his name Jesus for he shall save his people from their sin" (Matthew 1:21).

Prayer: Dear God in heaven, thank You for giving us Jesus, the Specialist who can forgive our sins. Teach us to know right from wrong. Forgive us when we sin against You. In Jesus' Name. Amen.

"No" Is an Answer

Pajama-clad, Sandy and Todd watched the pelting rain from their upstairs bedroom window. It was a heavy rain. It beat against the window pane like sharp, noisy daggers. It made harsh splashy sounds as it hit the sidewalk pavement.

"Oh, dear," Sandy sighed. "We forgot to tell God today was the picnic."

"But I didn't forget," Todd told Sandy. "Right before I went to sleep I reminded God that today was the picnic."

"You did?" Sandy looked puzzled. "Did you tell Him He shouldn't let it rain?"

" 'Course. Why do you suppose I talked to Him about the picnic?"

Sandy wrinkled her forehead. Her lips shaped a pout.

"I can't understand it," she said. "Then why did He send the rain? I always thought God answers prayer."

"He does." It was Mother's voice. Sandy and Todd turned. They hadn't heard her come into the room.

"Come and sit with me on Sandy's bed," Mother invited. "Maybe I can explain."

When the children were settled on the bed Mother said, "When you ask me for things, do I always say 'yes'?"

The children laughed. They knew she didn't.

" 'Course not," Todd said.

"If I remember right," Mother said. "A few days ago you asked me if you could go with Dad to the country. Now I knew how much you would like to go. But Dad had special work to do at the Benson farm. He had several other calls to make that day, too. Your being with him would have hindered his work. So I said. . . ."

" 'No,' " Sandy ended the sentence for her mother.

"Was that 'no' an answer to your asking to go with your father?"

The children nodded.

"Now I had a reason for saying 'no.' Today Todd got a 'no' answer from God when he asked for sunny weather. God must have had some reason for sending the rain. Because He said

'no' to Todd's prayer doesn't mean that He didn't hear it."

Something to Think About: Too often children think God only says "yes" when they pray. They forget "no" is an answer, too. And this we should remember. A "no" answer doesn't mean God doesn't hear. It means He chooses to answer that way.

But here is a happy thought. God always says "yes" to prayers that ask forgiveness.

Bible Verse: "Give ear, Oh Lord, to my prayer. . . . in the day of trouble I will call, for you will answer" (Psalm 86:6, 7).

Prayer: Dear God, we thank You because You do hear our prayers. Please do for us what You know is best. In Jesus' Name. Amen.

Learn to Follow

Johnny slammed his books on the table.

"*Johnny, pick up your clothes. Johnny, close that door. Johnny, study your lesson. Johnny, do this. Johnny, do that.* That's all I ever hear around here."

Johnny Simms was in a bad mood.

Calmly, patiently, Mother listened to him. When he finally got himself settled to begin his homework, Mother spoke.

"Sounds as though you don't like being told what to do."

"I don't!" Johnny answered. "Just once I'd like to do as I please."

Mother didn't say any more until Johnny had finished his lessons. Then she went to the table and sat down beside him. She placed a piece of string on the table in front of him. The piece of string was about a foot long.

"Johnny," she said. "I want to show you something. Put your finger on one end of the string and push it toward me."

Johnny did as his mother said. But the string didn't move very far. It just bunched up on the table.

"Now pull the string toward you," Mother told Johnny.

Johnny pulled the string across the table. It straightened out and followed where he pulled.

"Johnny, you are like that string. Tonight you felt you were being pushed around when you were told what to do. Then you bunched yourself up in an angry mood.

"The better way is to learn to follow just as the string followed your hand when you pulled it across the table.

"Dad and I want the very best life for you. If we let you do as you please, you wouldn't grow up to be the kind of person we want our son to be. Everyone needs someone to lead and show him the right way to go."

Something to Think About: Who are some of the people you must learn to follow? Why?

Jesus said, "I must do the will of my Father." When He said these words, He showed us that we must also learn to do God's will.

Bible Verse: "Search me, O God, and know my heart, try me and know my thoughts. See if there be any wicked way in me and *lead* me in the way everlasting" (Psalm 139:23, 24).

Prayer: Dear Lord, search our hearts today. Point out the things that are evil. Help us to obey those who are over us. Keep our thoughts clean and pure and lead us in paths that are everlasting. In Thy Name. Amen.

Who Will Be in Heaven?

"Mother, who will be in heaven?" Scott asked one bright sunny day as he watched her weed the garden.

Mother looked up from her weeding.

"Who will be in heaven?" Mother repeated the question. "Hmmmmm, let's see." Scott knew this meant she was thinking what to tell him.

"You know I believe this garden has the answer for you," Mother told him after awhile. "Let's look at it." She pointed to the plants she had been weeding.

"What plants are these?" she asked.

"Carrots," Scott answered. He knew because he had eaten them.

"And these?" she asked, pointing to a different row.

"Onions."

"And these?" Mother asked again.

"Corn?" Scott answered quickly.

"Why do carrots grow in one place, onions in another, and corn over there?" Mother asked.

Scott grinned. That was a foolish question for Mother to ask. Everyone should know that.

"Because that's what was planted," Scott said.

"True," Mother told him. "And this is the thing you should remember. Like seeds, people die and are buried in the ground. If they belong to Jesus when they die, they will belong to Him when they are raised from the dead. God has said this is so. So, the people who go to heaven will be the ones who love Jesus here on earth."

Something to Think About: Just as the old seed dies in the ground, our bodies will disappear and we will get new bodies for heaven. We will be with Jesus forever if we loved and served Him when we lived on earth.

Bible Verse: "Not everyone who says, Lord, Lord, shall enter into heaven, just those who do the will of their Father in heaven" (Matthew 7:21).

Prayer: Dear Jesus, we thank You because You are the Resurrection and Life. We know no one will come to the Father but by You. Help us to love You always so that when You come to get us we will be ready to go to heaven. In Thy dear Name. Amen.

Brighten the Corner Where You Are

Paul's Sunday school class didn't have a special room in which to meet. The teacher had tried having class in the main church sanctuary. But there were other classes there and the children found it hard to hear her.

She decided she would hunt for a place where her class could meet by itself. And she found one!

It wasn't a very fancy place. It was just a corner under the stairway that led into the basement.

But it would do, she said. She hung a curtain to shut off the corner from the rest of the hall. Then she moved her desk and the children's chairs into the little stairway corner.

The first time Paul's class met in this new room, the superintendent of the Sunday school stopped by to see how they were getting along.

"Well," he said, "I see you are brightening the corner where you are."

Paul's teacher thought that was a wonderful greeting.

"Things may not always be so nice in life," she said. "But we can brighten our corner wherever we are. Let's make the song about brightening the corner our theme song."

And that's exactly what they did.

Something to Think About: There are people who never seem to get discouraged. They are happy when they are sick. They are happy when they are poor. No matter what happens they praise God that He is their God.

We say these people have merry hearts. They brighten the corner where they are. And, because they do, they make other people happy, too.

Bible Verse: "A merry heart doeth good like medicine" (Proverbs 17:22).

Prayer: Dear Lord God, give me a merry heart. Help me to make others happy, too. Help me to brighten my corner wherever it is. In Jesus' blessed Name. Amen.

Spoiled Appetites

"Sally," Mother said, "why aren't you eating?"

Sally put her fork down on her plate. How could she tell her mother she wasn't hungry? Mother had prepared all the things Sally liked best — chicken with dumplings, new peas, jello salad, and yummy apple pie.

Oh, Sally thought, *how I wish I hadn't eaten that candy.*

"I'm not hungry," she told her mother.

"Not hungry!" Mother asked in a very surprised tone of voice. "That's strange. An hour ago you said you were starved."

Mother looked at Sally closely. Sally picked up her fork and began to peck at her food. Mother reached over and felt Sally's forehead.

"You aren't sick, are you?" she asked.

Sally looked up from her plate, very much ashamed.

"No," she said. "I'm not hungry because I ate all the candy Aunt Jane sent me."

Something to Think About: Candy is good in its place. Too much of it at the wrong time is bad. It steals our appetite for good, nourishing food that helps build strong bodies.

There are many things that steal our appetite for good things.

Children who read comic books all the time soon find they have lost their appetite for good books.

Children who watch horror pictures on television soon find they have no appetite for good programs.

Bad companions spoil one's appetite for good companions. Bad habits spoil the taste for good habits.

Can you name other things that ruin a child's appetite for things that are good?

Bible Verse: "Evil companions (playmates) corrupt (spoil) good manners" (I Corinthians 15:33).

Prayer: Dear Father in heaven, keep us from things that spoil our appetite for what is good. Help us always to choose what is best for our lives. In Jesus' Name. Amen.

On the Broad Way

Karen Sue, Mother, and Aunt Nell were driving into the city to shop.

Aunt Nell helped Mother watch the street signs so they would know where to go.

"We should reach Broadway very soon," Aunt Nell told Mother.

"Broadway!" Karen Sue almost shouted the word. There was fear in her voice. "Not broad way . . . we don't ever want to be on broad way."

Mother and Aunt Nell couldn't understand why Karen Sue feared Broadway. It was a big street that led through the shopping part of the city.

Mother decided she would find out.

"Why don't you want us to drive on Broadway?" she asked.

" 'Cause our Sunday school teacher said that is the way to destruction. . . . that is the wrong way. . . . we'll never get to heaven on the broad way."

Something to Think About: Now Mother understood. In the Bible the sinful way is called the broad (wide) way because it leaves room for all kinds of sin.

The right way is called the "narrow" way because it hasn't room for sin.

Karen Sue knew this. She didn't realize "Broadway" was the real name of a fine city street. When Mother explained, she understood.

"But, honey," Mother told Karen Sue, "we'll always stay away from Satan's 'broad' way — you can be sure of that."

Bible Verse: ". . . Broad is the way that leads to destruction . . . but narrow is the way that leads to life everlasting" (Matthew 7:13, 14).

Prayer: Dear Jesus, help us to find the narrow, straight way that leads to heaven. Keep us from traveling on the broad way where sin is found. In Your Name. Amen.

God Knows His Children

Paula was a good "pretender." She liked to dress up in Mother's old clothes. All dressed up, she would pretend she was Mrs. Tumbleweed or Mrs. Pinecroft.

Mother was never surprised when Mrs. Tumbleweed or Mrs. Pinecroft came to call.

"Come in, come in!" she would tell dressed-up Paula. "And whom do I have the pleasure of greeting this fine Monday morning?"

"I'm Mrs. Pinecroft, your new neighbor," Paula would say, adjusting the dad-sized glasses she wore. "I just thought I'd drop in and chat awhile."

Mrs. Pinecroft, Mother learned, had six children. What a merry time they gave their mother. Mr. Pinecroft was the mayor of the town, the new mill owner, or the chief of police — whatever Paula decided that day he would be.

One day, just for fun, Mother decided she'd be a pretender, too. So, when the door bell rang, she hurried to open the door.

"A salesman," Mother acted very much surprised. "Hello there," she said. "I'm sorry, sir, but I don't need anything today." She started to close the door.

Paula put out her hand.

"Mother," she began, "don't . . ."

But Mother wasn't listening.

"I'm sorry, sir. I don't need a thing. I have all the brooms I want. I have all the brushes I want. I don't need any spices. No, I'm sorry. . . ." she began to close the door again.

This time Paula grabbed Mother's arm.

"Don't you know me, Mother?" she asked. There were real tears in her voice. Mother looked down at Paula. Paula's lip trembled.

Then right away, Mother changed. She stooped down and scooped Paula into her arms, old clothes, dad-sized glasses and all.

"Of course I know you," she said. "I was only pretending. I'd know you anywhere. Aren't you my own little girl?"

148

Something to Think About: Do you blame Paula for being frightened when Mother pretended she didn't know her? That would be a frightening thing, wouldn't it?

But remember this is just a story. Some day people are going to knock at heaven's door. It is going to be very important how God greets them.

According to the Bible He will tell some who knock, "Go away, I don't know you. You aren't My children."

To others He will say, "Come, ye blessed of the Father. This is My kingdom prepared for you."

In which group will you be?

Bible Verse: "Be ye therefore followers of God, as dear children" (Ephesians 5:1).

Prayer: We thank You, our Heavenly Father, that we can be Your children. Help us to be obedient children. Help us to keep Your commandments always. In Thy Son's Name. Amen.

Fill the Gap

One day when Mother and Dad, Mary and Dean were traveling in northern Minnesota, they decided to have dinner in a cafeteria. They thought they could be served faster that way Also, they could see their food before they decided what they wanted to eat.

Mother and Dad, Mary and Dean lined up with the other people to get their food. Each person picked up his own tray, silverware, and a napkin. Then he moved down the line to choose the food that was being offered that day.

Suddenly Dean left his place in the line and stepped ahead of three or four women.

When they were eating, Dad asked why he did this.

"Didn't you see the sign?" Dean asked. "There by the wall." He pointed to a large sign painted on the wall. It said, "IF THERE IS A GAP IN THE LINE STEP UP AND FILL IT."

"There was a gap in the line, so I stepped up and filled it," Dean told his father.

Something to Think About: Dad told Dean he had done the right thing. He said that was the way it is in life, too. Some people hold back a line. And some people don't take their places where they should. Sometimes there are gaps in the work that needs to be done for the Lord.

God needs people to sing in the choir. He needs Sunday school teachers. He needs boys and girls to invite folks to come to church. He needs people to give part of their money to the Lord. Those who do not fill their place leave a gap that needs to be filled.

Dad told Dean and Mary he hoped they would always step forward and fill such gaps when they saw them.

Bible Verse: "Whatsoever thy hand findeth to do, do with all thy might" (Ecclesiastes 9:10).

Prayer: Dear Heavenly Father, thank You for giving us work to do for You. Help us to see the things that we can do. Make us willing to fill gaps left by other people. Keep us this day. In Jesus' Name. Amen.

The Dead Mouse

Mother and Daddy had gone on a long trip. While they were gone, Grandmother came to stay with Brent and Randy.

One day Grandmother looked out the kitchen window. To her surprise she saw Brent and Randy playing with a dead mouse. She opened the window.

"Brent! Randy!" she called. "Where did you get that mouse?"

"Jimmy's cat killed it," Brent told her.

"Well, get rid of it!" she said. "Sometimes mice carry disease germs." Then thinking fast she said, "Say, I know what you can do. Why don't you dig a hole in the ground and bury the mouse?"

"Let's!" the boys cried. That sounded like a great idea.

Grandmother watched the boys dig a hole near some flowers in the garden. She watched them put the mouse in the hole and cover it with dirt.

Satisfied, Grandmother went back to her work.

152

About an hour later she called the boys to come in for their naps. To her surprise she found they were playing with the mouse again.

"I thought I told you to bury the mouse," she said.

"We did," Randy told her.

"Is that a different mouse?" Grandmother asked.

"Oh, no, it's the same one. Only we didn't bury its tail," Randy told her. "We wanted to be able to find it again."

Something to Think About: Brent and Randy obeyed Grandmother, partly, not altogether. They got rid of the mouse. But they made sure it would be easy to find again.

That's the way some people do with sin. God shows them what is wrong. They promise to get rid of it. And they do, partly. They hang on to a little bit of it and soon they are right back where they started.

God wants us to get rid of all of the sin in our lives, not just a little part of it.

Bible Verse: "Whosoever does not forsake (leave) all sin cannot be my disciple" (Luke 14:33).

Prayer: Dear Heavenly Father, we know that You hate sin. We know, too, that You love all people even though they sin. We know You want them to turn from their sin. Help us to leave all sin for Your sake. In Jesus' Name. Amen.

The Forgotten Flashlight

Mother looked up from the book she was reading. Her son, John, had just come into the room.

"Why, John," she said. "How does it happen you are home? Didn't you go to the cave?"

John put his bag lunch on the table. Mother could tell something was wrong. About an hour earlier John had left to join the boys in his Sunday school class. Their teacher had told them he had found a cave in a hill on his farm. Together they were going to explore the cave. And now John was home.

"Didn't you go to the cave?" Mother asked the question again.

"Sure. But I couldn't go in. I forgot my flashlight."

"Couldn't you have shared someone's?" Mother asked.

"No. That wouldn't work. The path into the cave is narrow and very steep. Each person had to have his own light."

"Oh, that's too bad," Mother said. "Did any of the others forget their flashlights?"

"Karl and Tom," John answered unhappily. "Now we have to wait until next Saturday."

Something to Think About: John didn't fare so badly. He had another chance to visit the cave. The Bible tells us this won't be true when we come to enter heaven. If we don't have the right light, we will be turned away. The right light means Jesus Christ, of course.

To make this truth plain, Jesus told a story about ten women who were on their way to a wedding. Five of them forgot to put oil in their lamps. When they went to buy oil, the bridegroom came and they missed the wedding.

Are you ready to meet Jesus when He comes again?

Bible Verse: "Watch therefore (be ready) for you do not know the hour when your Lord will come" (Matthew 24:42).

Prayer: Dear Lord, we thank You for these stories that warn us to be ready when You come. Help us to live each day as good followers of Yours. In Jesus' Name. Amen.

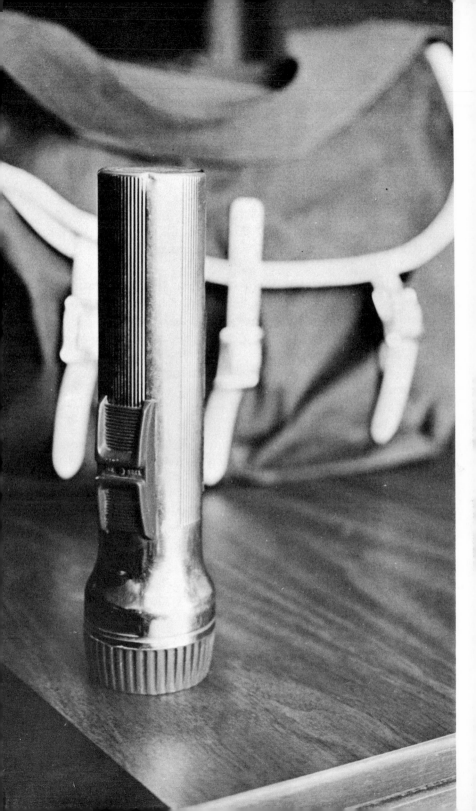

Was Lowell Lost?

Lowell had taken his tricycle and made his way over the bridge a few blocks from his home. Down below the bridge were railroad tracks. On the tracks were railroad cars. And near the cars were large pens where cows, sheep and pigs waited to be shipped to far away cities.

Lowell loved to watch the animals. He had been here many times with his mother and father.

He steered his tricycle down the hill and went over to the fence where he could see the cows, sheep and pigs without getting hurt.

After he had been there for a long time he remembered he hadn't had his lunch. He'd better go home, he thought. He pulled his tricycle up the hill and started home.

The first thing he knew a car pulled up alongside of the sidewalk where he was riding. His father was driving the car.

"Where have you been?" his father asked. "We've been looking all over for you. Mother was worried when she found you were lost."

Lowell shook his head.

"I wasn't lost, Daddy," he said. "I was watching the animals. I knew how to get home. Don't you remember you and Mother had showed me the way?"

Something to Think About: Did you know that heaven is often spoken of as being our eternal (everlasting) home? The time we spend here is very short compared to the time we shall spend in our heavenly home.

Now, God was good to Lowell in giving him a father and mother who had showed him the way to his everyday home. But, he was still more blessed because his father and mother had taught him the way to the heavenly home. Lowell knew he must believe and trust in Jesus Christ to reach that home.

Bible Verse: "I am the way," Jesus said, "the truth and the life. No man comes to the Father but by me" (John 14:6).

Prayer: Dear Lord, thank You for those who have showed us the way to our heavenly home. Thank You for our Sunday school teachers. Thank You for our pastor. Thank You for our mothers and fathers. Thank You, too, for the Bible that tells us about Your Son, Jesus Christ.

Be with us this day. Keep us well and strong and keep our minds fixed on what You would have us do. In Jesus' Name. Amen.

The Scar Story

Dennis looked at his father as if he had never seen him before.

"What's the matter, son?" his father asked.

"Oh, that scar on your face. I never noticed it before. Where did you get it? Was it an accident? How did it happen?"

Father ran his hand over a long rough mark on the side of his face.

"I'm not very proud of that," he told Dennis. "I'd like to forget it is there. But, every day when I wash and shave my face I remember what happened to me when I was a boy about your age."

"Well, what did happen?" Dennis asked. He was really curious now.

Father touched the scar again.

"This scar came to me because I didn't mind my mother. When I was little we lived on a farm. We had a stove in which we burned wood. One day when I came in from playing I smelled something cooking on the stove. It smelled like sweet chocolate candy.

"I wanted to see if it was candy so I moved a kitchen chair over by the stove. This was something mother had told me never to do. I was just ready to climb up on the chair when mother called from the other room. She had heard me move the chair.

" 'Charles! Stay away from the stove.'

"Well, the chair was there, and all I had to do was climb up on it. If I hurried I could see the candy and get down before she came back into the kitchen. At least that is what I thought.

"I put one foot up on the chair. I moved quickly. I'll never know how it happened, but before I knew it, the chair tipped and I fell against the hot stove."

Father touched the scar on his face.

"I burned my cheek badly. That's why I have the scar."

"Was Grandmother mad?" Dennis asked.

"I don't believe she was as angry as she was sorry I hadn't obeyed her. I can still remember how lovingly she took care of the burn. All I did was cry. But between sobs I told her I was

sorry and asked her to forgive me.

"Dennis, you know Grandmother well enough to know she was happy to forgive me. Just the same the scar is still there. You see we can't sin without it leaving some mark on our body or soul."

Something to Think About: The story father told Dennis is a lesson for all boys and girls. Can you tell why?

Here is another question. Suppose Dennis' father hadn't fallen against the stove. Would what he did still be called sin? Why?

Bible Verse: "Be sure your sin will find you out" (Numbers 32:23).

Prayer: Dear Lord and Heavenly Father, we come to You today thankful for all that You have given us. Thank You for our parents. Thank You for our brothers and sisters. Thank You for food and clothing. Thank You for our home.

Help us today to be obedient children. Help us to mind those who are supposed to take care of us. Help us to remember that You see everything we do. Forgive us for the times when we have sinned. In Jesus' Name. Amen.

It's Free!

Nan snuggled down in her chair, happy that she had come to the children's meeting. Daddy's friend, Jim Browne, a missionary, was going to talk about the boys and girls he had known in Africa.

Nan liked Jim Browne. Daddy had often said he was the best missionary he knew.

When the children had finished singing, the leader introduced Jim to Nan's friends.

Nan smiled. She sat up straight and got ready to listen. She hoped he would tell about an elephant hunt or something like that.

But he didn't. Just before he began to speak he did something that seemed very strange to Nan. He reached into his pocket and took out a coin. He held it up so everyone could see it.

"It's a quarter," he said. He walked over to a table nearby. "I'm going to put it on the table. Now," he went on, "I want you to know this quarter is free to anyone who comes and gets it."

The boys and girls looked at each other, surprised. Did he really mean what he said, they wondered. "I think he's only fooling," the girl who sat next to Nan whispered in her ear.

Nan didn't answer. She didn't know what to think. It wasn't like Jim Browne to fool anyone. But to go and get the quarter. She didn't think she wanted to do that. What if he put his hand over it when she was ready to pick it up? She'd surely feel foolish then.

No one moved. Jim pointed to the quarter again. "I mean it," he said. "I'm going to tell you about the boys and girls in Africa and if anyone wants to come and get the quarter while I'm speaking you may do so. It's yours. All you have to do is take it."

Nan didn't know what made her do it. But quick as a flash she slid off her chair and walked to where Jim was standing. She reached out and took the quarter.

Jim put his arm around her.

"Good girl, Nan," he said. "I guess the other boys and girls didn't believe me when I said they could have the quarter. Why

161

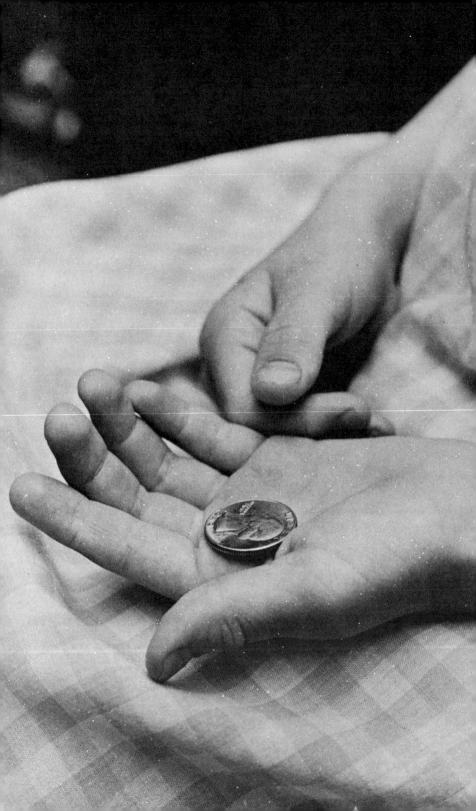

did you believe me?"

Nan smiled at Jim.

"Because I knew you wouldn't fool us," she said.

"That's right," he said. "And today I'm going to tell you about Someone else who wouldn't fool you. Can you guess who He is?"

Something to Think About: Nan knew that Jim meant Jesus. She was right. Jim told the boys and girls that Jesus was God's free gift to all people. Anyone, old or young, can have Him as a Friend and Saviour.

When Jim spoke about the boys and girls he had known in Africa, he said he had tried the same thing with them. Then he used a pocket knife instead of a quarter. The boy who came to get the knife could hardly believe it was his to keep. But Jim said it was.

When Jim told him he could have Jesus for a Friend and Saviour the boy said,

"I want Him, too."

Nan had already asked Jesus to come into her heart so she knew what Jim said was true.

Bible Verse: "For God so loved the world, that he gave his only begotten Son, that whosoever believeth in him should not perish, but have everlasting life" (John 3:16).

Prayer: Thank You for Your great love, dear Lord. Thank You for sending Your Son, Jesus Christ, as a free gift so that everyone who believes in Him can have everlasting life. Help us to love You always. In Jesus' Name. Amen.

Prove It

Cowboy Jim was talking about some people he had known who said they loved God.

"Too often they didn't do anything to show that love," he said. "Let me tell you what I mean.

"Suppose I sat around the ranch and sang songs of praise to my boss. Suppose I kept bragging to other people, telling them what a great guy he is.

"Suppose I told him how much I liked to work for him, then stayed in bed until all the chores were done.

"Do you think he would believe me? No siree! Without a second thought he'd send me packing. I wouldn't hold my job very long."

Then Cowboy Jim told how he *could* prove his love for his boss.

"I'd get out of bed when I was supposed to. I'd fix broken fences. I'd round up the cattle. I'd help brand the calves. I'd do everything I could to please the man who hired me. Only then would I really prove my love."

Something to Think About: There is a poem that tells about some children who said they loved their mother. But right after they told her they ran out to play leaving the work for her to do.

They didn't show their love very well, did they?

Boys and girls who make their beds without being told show mother they love her. So do those who help with the dishes without grumbling. And children who watch only the television programs mother and father say they should prove they love their parents, too.

How do you show your parents you love them?

How do you show God you love Him?

Bible Verse: "My little children, let us not love in word, neither in tongue; but in deed and in truth" (I John 3:18).

Prayer: Dear Lord Jesus, we do love You. We want You to know that we do. Help us to prove it by the things we do. Help us to be obedient and kind so our parents will know we love them, too. In Jesus' Name. Amen.

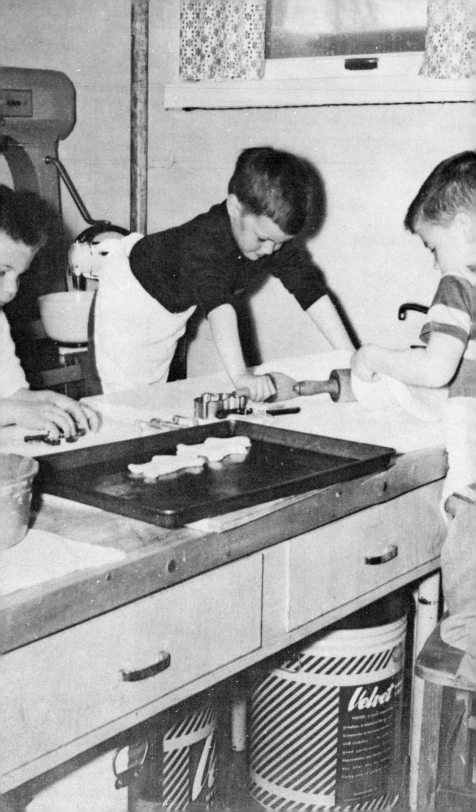

The Waterlogged Canoe

Jason lived on a farm near a lake. He loved the water and the green corn fields that grew right up to its very edge. He loved to hear the stories his father told about the country where the farm was located. He learned that long before his grandfather and grandmother had settled on the farm, Indians had camped along the lake shore. Jason knew this was true because he had found many Indian relics on the farm. He had found sharp pointed arrowheads. He had found what was left of stone toma- hawks. He had also found beads and broken pieces of Indian dishes.

Many people weren't able to find Indian beads and pieces of pottery. But Jason had trained his eyes so that when he walked along a corn row his eyes would spot them right away. When he walked along the lake shore he could tell when the sun shone on a stone whether it was an arrow tip or just a flat piece of stone.

One day as Jason walked along the side of the lake he made a strange discovery. The lake was crystal clear. Jason could see the bottom without any trouble at all. He saw the reeds that grew among the stones. He saw minnows dart back and forth between the reeds. Suddenly he stopped. *What was that?* he asked himself. It couldn't be, but it surely looked like a canoe. It was — a dug- out canoe like those used by Indians long ago.

Jason ran to tell his father. Father called neighbor Browne to come along.

After a lot of tugging and prying the canoe was loosened so it could be pulled to shore. It wasn't at all like the canoes we see today. It was really a log that had been scooped out to make a boat.

"Do you think it will float?" Jason wanted to know.

"I'm afraid not," Dad answered. "You see it's been soaked with water so long its wood is soft and spongy. I don't think it would ever dry out enough so it could float. When something gets soaked like that we say it is waterlogged. But I believe the state museum would be interested in seeing it."

That's where the canoe finally landed. And Jason was glad

because then many people could see how the Indians made their canoes.

And he'd almost forgotten he had ever found it until one day he heard his minister say that some Christians didn't do much for the Lord because they were *waterlogged* with things of this world. Then Jason thought about the canoe. It sank because it was waterlogged. No doubt people would sink, too, if they were waterlogged with sin.

Something to Think About: What does it mean to be waterlogged? How can a person be waterlogged with things of the world? A canoe is meant to ride on top of the water, isn't it? It is not meant to be filled with water. In the same way Christians are meant to live in the world but not to let the world fill them. What are the things you must be careful not to let become a part of your life?

Bible Verse: "Blessed are the pure in heart, for they shall see God" (Matthew 5:8).

Prayer: We thank You, dear God, because You have taught us to walk in the world without being a part of it. Show us the dangers we face as we go through life. Help us to keep our hearts and minds pure and clean that we might serve You as we should. Help us to choose which television programs to watch, which friends to make, which books to read. Don't let us become waterlogged by sin. In Jesus' Name, Amen.

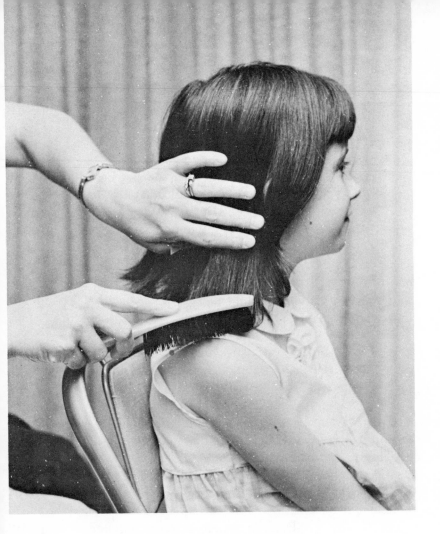

Counting by Ones

"Two, four, six, eight, ten, twelve. . . .

"Mommy, Mommy," Barbara called excitedly. "Listen. I can count by twos."

"That's nothing," her brother Tom said. "I can count by fives. Five, ten, fifteen, twenty, twenty-five, thirty. . . ."

Mother smiled and said, "You both do very well for your age. When you get older you will be able to count by sixes and sevens, eights and nines, too."

"Mother," Barbara began. "I just thought of something. How many can Jesus count by?"

Mother put her head to one side as she always did when she was thinking very hard. Suddenly she smiled broadly. "This is interesting," she said, "and I think it is the best thing I know about Jesus. He counts by ones."

"What do you mean?" Tom asked his mother.

"By ones?" Barbara asked, a puzzled look on her face.

"Yes, by ones. The Bible says so. It says He is interested in people not only by twos, threes, fours or even one hundreds, but *one by one*, too.

"When He talked about little children He said He didn't want a single one of them to be lost.

"When He told the story about the shepherd who had one hundred sheep, He said the shepherd went to look for *the one* that was lost.

"Another thing, Jesus said there is joy in heaven when *one* person turns from sin and asks Jesus to come into his heart."

Something to Think About: You like it when Mother and Father give you special attention, don't you? Aren't you glad that God knows all about each one of us, individually, and that He cares for us because He loves us *one by one?*

This is important to everyone who decides to live for Jesus. Each person must decide for Himself. You can't decide for someone else. And, someone else can't do it for you. Each of us comes to Jesus *one by one.*

Bible Verse: "Everyone shall give an account of himself" (Romans 14:12).

Prayer: Dear Jesus, we are glad that You fed a crowd of many thousand people. But we are glad that You love and care for each one of us, too. Help us to love others as You love us. May we be kind, loving and honest so that we can please You. Guide each one of us today. Amen.

170

Kathy's Home Now

Bill and Betty were very sad. Their best friend, Kathy, who had been sick for so long, had died. Until Kathy left them, they had never had a close friend their age who had died. It was hard for them to understand that she would never come to play with them again.

At supper Bill asked about Kathy.

"I don't think we ought to feel badly because she left us," Mother said. "She's home now."

"Home?" The word was like a question. It was Betty who asked it.

"Yes, home." This time Father spoke. "Do you remember the song Grandmother used to sing so often?" he asked. "The name of it was 'Heaven Is My Home.' "

"I remember," Betty told her father. "And she used to talk about going home. I had forgotten all about it . . . until now."

"I know you miss Kathy," Mother told Bill and Betty. "But, you can be sure of this. She's happy where she is. She won't have any more pain. Best of all, you will see her someday."

"I still can't see how she could think heaven was her home," Bill offered.

"Well, look at it this way," Mother explained. "Do you remember when we moved here from the West Coast? We traveled for days and days. Then when we got here there was no house ready for us to move into."

"We lived in a motel, didn't we?" Bill asked. "It seemed like we stayed there for years and years, but I know it wasn't."

"Yes, and I'll never forget the day we moved into this house. Bill, you came rushing in from the car. You looked around as if you couldn't believe you were really here. Then you threw your cap into the air and shouted, 'Bill's home now!'"

"Did I? I don't remember that."

"Yes, you did. And I'd like to think that when Kathy went to be with God, she said, 'Kathy's home now.'"

Something to Think About: Many people say death is like the experience a butterfly has when it leaves its dead cocoon. In death the body is left, but the spirit (the part that belongs to God) wings its way to be with Him.

The apostle Paul talked about death a good deal. He was not afraid to die. He said as long as he lived he would live for Christ, but when he died he would be far better off because then he would be with the Lord.

Bible Verse: ". . . for we have a place with God, a building not made with hands, eternal in the heavens" (II Corinthians 5:1).

Prayer: Dear Heavenly Father. Thank You for preparing a place for us to go when we die. Thank You for sending Your Son to earth so that those of us who believe in Him can meet Him some day. Keep us true to You. Help us live so others will learn to love Him, too. Amen.

Christmas Is for Giving

Karen had so many toys she didn't know which to choose when she wanted to play. She had several dolls. Her closet was full of lovely clothes. In fact, Karen had so much she forgot many children have very little.

Karen knew Christmas was coming. She began thinking about the gifts she would like to receive. She thought and thought. But she couldn't decide. *I'll ask Mother to help me,* she said to herself.

"Mother," Karen said one day, "tell me what I want for Christmas?"

Something to Think About: Karen had forgotten one of the most important things about Christmas. Do you know what it is?

Karen had forgotten that *Christmas is for giving.*

Christmas is Christ's birthday. And because the wisemen brought Him gifts after He was born people give gifts now when they celebrate His birthday.

There are several things that we should remember when we give gifts. First, we should give to those from whom we don't expect any gifts. Give just for the fun of giving.

Give toys to someone who has very few or none.

Give food to people who are hungry.

Give money to your church to send to help people in other lands.

Be sure you give something to Jesus on His birthday. It can be a gift of money that you give for the church to use for Him. It can be a promise to love and serve Him better.

The best gift, of course, is to give Him your heart. Then, as you grow older, you will want to give Him your time, your money, your voice . . . everything that you are and have.

Bible Verse: ". . . they first gave their own selves to the Lord" (II Corinthians 8:5).

Prayer: Dear Heavenly Father, thank You for sending Jesus to this earth. Thank You for Christmas when we celebrate His birthday. Help us to remember that Christmas is for giving. Make us willing to give Jesus all of our life. Amen.

In Your Own Words

"Dean!" Mrs. Handerson called as she left the garden and started toward the house. "Dean!" she called again.

I wonder where he is, she thought to herself.

All at once she realized she hadn't seen him for a long time. "Dean!" She raised her voice.

But Dean didn't answer.

Mrs. Handerson went into the house. Just as she stepped into the kitchen Dean came through the hallway door that led to his bedroom.

"Did you call me?" he asked.

"Yes, I did," his mother answered. "Where were you?"

"I was in my room."

"And what were you doing there?"

"I was praying for Pastor Chalmers."

"Oh, I'm so glad," Mrs. Handerson told Dean. Pastor Chalmers was a very sick man. Everyone had been asked to pray for him. It pleased her to know that Dean had been praying for him. It pleased her still more when Dean said, "I thought of the words all by myself."

Something to Think About: Often we pray prayers that someone has taught us. But, there are times when the words of these prayers don't seem to fit what we want to say. That's when we ought to think up words for prayers of our own.

You can do this if you talk to God as you would to a very dear friend. Tell Him you love Him. Tell Him about your friends who are ill. Ask Him to do what is best for them. Be sure of this, He will listen to you when you pray.

Bible Verse: "They talked to the Lord about their troubles and he heard them" (Psalm 107:6).

Prayer: Dear Lord Jesus, we are glad that we can talk to You as we do to our parents and friends. We want to thank You for listening to us when we pray.

Bless our pastor today. Keep him well and strong. Be with our missionaries. Keep them well and strong, too. We ask in Your blessed Name. Amen.

It's Your Problem

When Scott came to live in the Jensen home, Mother and Father Jensen were very happy. They had prayed and hoped for a baby boy for such a long time. Scott was a pretty baby, too. And, in just a few years he grew to be quite a handsome child.

But Scott had one very bad fault. He didn't always obey his mother. He loved to play with his little cars. He loved to play with his trucks. He loved to play with his toy soldiers. But when he was through playing he didn't want to put his toys back in the box where they belonged.

One day Scott's mother said, "Scott, if you don't pick up your toys I'll get cross and cranky, you know. You wouldn't want Mother to be cross and cranky, would you?"

Scott looked at her quietly. Then he said, "Well, that's your problem, I guess."

Something to Think About: Scott really didn't mean to be naughty when he answered his mother as he did. But, what he said seems very much as though he were trying to be *"smart."*

What he forgot was that it wasn't only his mother's problem. If Mother became cross and had to scold it was because *he* hadn't done what he was told to do.

Think about this for awhile. Soon you'll realize that when other people act unfriendly, cross or sad it may be because you did something to make them feel that way.

Instead of blaming them for the way they behave, let's begin asking ourselves how we behave to them. *That's our problem.*

Bible Verse: "Thus said the Lord, Consider your ways (consider what you do)" (Haggai 1:7).

Prayer: Dear Heavenly Father, thank You for our home. Thank You for our family. Thank You for sending Jesus to be our Friend. Help us today to watch what we do . . . to consider our ways. We don't want anyone to get out of sorts because of what we do. In Jesus' Name. Amen.

The Best Nickname

Boyd's family had just moved to the new town. When Boyd had been in the new school for about a week, his father asked,

"Well, Boyd, have you made a lot of new friends?"

Boyd nodded. At least he had learned to know who some of the boys were. And he hoped they'd be his friends.

"So far I like *Stretch* best of all," he told his father.

"*Stretch?* Say, that's a funny name."

Boyd laughed.

"Oh, that's not really his name," he said. "His real name is Karl, but all the kids call him Stretch."

"Why?"

"Well, I think it's because he's a lot shorter than the rest of the fellows. I guess the kids think he needs to stretch."

Father smiled.

"That's what we call a nickname," he said. "And, sometimes a nickname tells a good deal more about a person than his real name does. Why, when I was in school I had a friend we always called *Snail*. Know why?"

"Was he slow as a snail?" Boyd asked, feeling good because he was sure he had guessed why.

"That's why," Father said. "No matter where we went we always had to wait for him."

"There was a kid called *Fatso* in our other school."

"Say, that reminds me," Father said. "Did you know there were nicknames in Bible times, too?"

"Honest?" Boyd hadn't known this was true.

Father picked up the Bible that lay on a nearby table. He opened it to a verse in the book of Acts. Then he asked Boyd to read it.

Boyd read, "'. . . And the disciples were called Christians first in Antioch.' Was *Christian* a nickname?" he asked.

"Yes, it was," Father answered. "And it means just exactly what it says . . . *'Christ men.'* Why do you suppose the disciples were nicknamed Christians by the people in Antioch?"

Boyd thought awhile. Then he answered, "They must have

178

he had found him, he brought him
Ăn'tĭŏçh. For a whole year they m
withʲ the church, and taught a lar
company of people; and in Antioch t
disciples were for the first time call
Christians.

ow in these days prophets can
om Jerusalem to Ăn'tĭŏç
e of them named Ăg'ăb
nd foretold by the Spirit th
ld be a great famine over
d; and this took place in t
Claudius. ²⁹And the discipl
ined, every one according to
ty, to send relief to the brethr
o lived in Judē'ă; ³⁰ and they did s
ending it to the elders by the hand
Bar'năbăs and Saul.

James killed; Peter imprisoned

12 About that time Hĕrŏd the kir
laid violent hands upon son
who belonged to the church. ² H
killed James the brother of John wi
the sword; ³ and when he saw that

lived so people could tell they belonged to Jesus."

"Right," Father said as he closed the Bible, "and the nickname lasted. That's why followers of Jesus are still called *Christians.*"

Something to Think About: Suppose we had moved to Antioch with the early disciples. Even though we had names like Mary, Jane, Bob, Paul and Peter, would the people have called us Christians because we were so much like Jesus?

Perhaps you are wondering if Boyd's friends can tell that he belongs to Jesus, that he is a "Christ man."

How about you?

Bible Verse: "Then Jesus said to those Jews which believed on him, If ye continue in my word (if you obey my word), then are ye my disciples indeed" (John 8:31).

Prayer: Dear Lord, we thank You for the Bible that tells us how the early Christians lived. We thank You that they proved to others that they belonged to You. Help us to remember to live up to the name Christian, too. In Jesus' Name. Amen.

Happy Day

One day in January Sally Lou began thinking about a trip her family had taken shortly before Christmas.

She remembered that she and her sisters had shopped for gifts for Mother and Father. They had visited the toy department of a big store. Then, on the way home, they had stopped at a restaurant to have dinner. This was a real treat because Father often didn't have money enough for the whole family to eat in a restaurant.

Sally Lou couldn't remember for sure where they had eaten so she decided to ask her mother.

"Mother, did we eat at the *Light House* when we came back from Minneapolis?"

"Yes, we did," Mother said.

"And, did we have chicken?" Sally Lou wanted to know.

"Yes, we all ordered chicken."

Sally Lou's lip drooped. Suddenly she began to cry.

"Whatever is the matter?" Mother asked.

Sally Lou looked at her mother sadly.

"But, I wanted *ham*," she said.

Something to Think About: Mother couldn't help but laugh when Sally Lou said she wanted ham.

"There's nothing to do about it, now," she told Sally Lou. "You just dry your tears and next time we eat out you make sure you order ham."

This story is very much like one about a little boy named Tom. One day Tom learned that his mother couldn't take him to the zoo the next day as she had planned. Right away he sat down and started to pout. When his father asked him what was troubling him he said,

"I can't go to the zoo."

"But, that's tomorrow, isn't it? Why be sad today about something that is going to happen tomorrow? Come, come, cheer up. Be happy today."

In the first story, Sally Lou was sad about something that had passed. In the second story Tom was sad about something

that hadn't yet happened. Both children were wrong in the way they behaved.

No one can go back and change what has happened. The best thing is to forget it. If it is something you did that was wrong, however, ask God to forgive you. Then go on to live today the best way you know how.

Nor does it pay to be unhappy about what might happen tomorrow. Things can change. But, even if they don't you mustn't be unhappy today about what might be tomorrow.

If we remember all the Lord has done for us we'll be happy today and every day.

Bible Verse: "This is the day which the Lord hath made, we will rejoice and be glad in it" (Psalm 118:24).

Prayer: Dear Heavenly Father, we thank You for giving us today. Help us to remember to be happy and cheerful in all that we do. In Jesus' Name. Amen.

Pages Have Stories

Mary Ann liked to talk about her home. At nursery school she told the other children what she did, what she ate and where she went with her father and mother. Best of all, she liked to talk about her church and Sunday school.

One day her teacher asked her what she did in Sunday school. "Oh, I sing and read."

"And, what do you read?"

"Oh, you know, pages, of course," Mary Ann said.

Something to Think About: Did Mary Ann's answer surprise you? Well, you can be sure she didn't mean what she said. It wasn't the pages but the stories on those pages that she liked so well.

Yet, when we think about it some more, what Mary Ann said is a lesson to us. Did you know you could listen to something without really hearing what was being read? Or you could read and not pay any attention to what you read. This happens sometimes when we go to church. We listen to the Bible . . . but we really don't hear what the preacher says. We sing the songs without thinking about the words.

This is wrong. Why? Because we go to church to worship God. God gave us ears to hear His Word.

Next time you go to church be sure you listen to what is being read; what is being sung; what is being said.

Bible Verse: "He who has ears, let him hear" (Matthew 11:15).

Prayer: Dear Lord, thank You for eyes to see all the beautiful things You have made. Thank You for ears to hear our mother and father speak. Thank You for ears to hear Thy Word. Help us to really listen when we worship You in our church. In Jesus' Name. Amen.

Person to Person

One summer Bobby and his sister Annette visited Yosemite National Park when they traveled through California with their father and mother.

Bobby liked the park. He liked the tall waterfall. He liked the big trees and the high mountain walls. Best of all he liked the deer that were everywhere. Some of them were very, very tame. One day a deer came right up to the picnic table and nibbled Bobby's sandwich.

Some days later, when Bobby, Annette, Mother and Father were driving along the highway on their way home, Bobby said,

"Do you know what? I know now why I liked the deer so much. That was the first time I had ever seen a deer *person to person.*"

Something to Think About: Have you ever felt as Bobby did? You've read about something. You've seen pictures and heard stories about it. But you really don't know all there is to know until you have seen the person, place, or thing for yourself.

This is true when you learn about Jesus, too.

You read stories about Him. You learn that He healed the sick. You know He loves little children. If you have given your life to Him, you know He is a very dear friend.

But, and this is a happy thought, some day you will know what He looks like. You will see Him as He really is because you will see Him "face to face" or "person to person" as Bobby would say.

Do you know where?

Bible Verse: "In my Father's house are many mansions, if it were not so I would have told you. I go to prepare a place for you. . . . that where I am there you may be also" (John 14:2, 3).

Prayer: Dear Lord and Heavenly Father, thank You for the Bible that tells us about Your Son, Jesus Christ. Thank You for Sunday school teachers who teach us about His love. Help us to live every day as He wants us to live. Thank You for promising us that we shall see Him some day. In His Name. Amen.

SCRIPTURE INDEX

Alum Rock Covenant Church
218 KIRK AVENUE
SAN JOSE 27, CALIFORNIA